AN ILLUSTRATED ACCIDENCE
AND GALLIMAUFRY OF THE
ANGLISH LINGUAGE

AN ILLUSTRATED ACCIDENCE

and Gallimaufry of the

ANGLISH LINGUAGE

EASIER TO USE, MORE COMPREHENSIVE, AND MORE AUTHORITATIVE THAN ANY OTHER.

Amassed and Illumed by
Samuel Zachariah Salant

THE MAIN STREET PRESS
Pittstown, New Jersey

All rights reserved

Copyright © 1987 by Samuel Zachariah Salant

No part of this book may be utilized or reproduced in any
form or by any means, electronic or mechanical, including
photocopying, recording, or by any information storage
and retrieval system, without permission in writing
from the publishers.

Published by
The Main Street Press
William Case House
Pittstown, New Jersey 08867

Published simultaneously in Canada by
Methuen Publications
2330 Midland Avenue
Agincourt, Ontario M1S 1P7

Printed in the United States of America

Library of Congress Cataloging-in-Publication Data

Salant, Samuel Zachariah.
   An illustrated accidence and gallimaufry of the anglish linguage /
amassed and illumed by Samuel Zachariah Salant.
   p.   cm.
   ISBN 1-55562-036-1
   1. Puns and punning. 2. English language—Anecdotes, facetiae,
satire, etc. I. Title.
PN6231.P8S24 1987
428.1'0207—dc 19   87-20992
                                                                 CIP

87 88 89 90 91 10 9 8 7 6 5 4 3 2 1

ADEFGHIKLMNOC
JPQRSTUVWXYZB

*To letters...without them,
this could not have been written,
and The Times would have been
"New York's Picture Newspaper."*

Precurse

In order to communicate with each other (since most of us lack the ability to read the minds of others), we use coded systems of mouth-produced noises, called 'words.' We can produce noises with other parts of our bodies as well, but these have no generally-understood meanings, and have certain side-effects which militate against their use, particularly in close surroundings.

But what if no one is there to hear these words? Then, we must find some way to preserve them so that, at some later time, a person with the proper decoding ability would be able to retrieve what had originally been coded into words.

Just as there are many word-codes in use, (called 'linguages,' after the Latin *lingua*, as in the words *lingua franca*, which means 'French money talks'), so there are differing ways to preserve them; all are sensoral: some are aural, such as recordings on disc or tape; some are of a tactile nature, like Braille notation; still others are visual (dirty pictures or other patterns upon a surface, assembled in an agreed-upon manner, to correspond to our mouth-produced noises). We will not deal with dirty pictures here; the more pruriently-inclined may indulge their disgusting vice in the perusal of 'The Official Sex Manual,' a publication of G.P.Putnam's Sons, 1965 (Library of Congress Catalog Card Number 65-20689), fortunately long out of print.

Now, as to these surface patterns: they are called *letters*, which is a word derived through the Old French from the Latin *littera*, whence we get our 'literature,' our 'literati,' and, as a natural result, our 'litter.' The concern of this compendium is primarily with these letters, rather than with the words into which they assemble, although there will be a few words used, as needed, for illustrative purposes. The general reader may ignore them, should he find them interrupting the smooth flow of the ideas presented herein.

Forewarn

Many have wondered about the letters of the alphabet. They ask, "Where did they come from?" Now that question can be answered with absolute certainty. Many have claimed to have been first: The Chinese believe that Ts'ang Chien invented letters. They also believe that he had four eyes and the face of a dragon, so *that* doesn't seem very likely. The Indians (of India) say that the god Brahma made letters in the patterns of the seams in the human skull, which is all very well, but it is obvious that he used an *Indian* skull, because all the other alphabets are completely different.

We can dismiss the Irish legend of Ogmios, and also the claims of the Nordic god, Odin, because they dealt in *runes* (which went out of fashion almost immediately), and that of the Assyrian god Nebo too, for they were a dead end: they were an expression of words, not letters, and it is the letters we are after, in the final analysis.

The Egyptians *were* a lettered people. Unfortunately, their letters were interlaced with pictures (most of which were not *too* dirty, which is quite surprising when one considers that incest was the national sport). Their writing-system was invented by the god Thoth, who had the head of a bird, which may explain why pictures and letters were all mixed together. Still, they *had* letters, some of which were stolen by people who called themselves Phoenicians. These Phoenicians escaped with the letters and set up a country of their own, which they used as a base for their far-ranging trading operations (but that is another story). If we examine the name *Phoenician* carefully, it becomes clear that *they* invented letter-sounds! The word 'phonetic' obviously refers to them, as does the word 'phoney,' which is probably a reference to their sharp business practices.

There is one more piece of evidence: the Greeks say that Cadmus, their national hero, brought back at least sixteen letters from Phoenicia. It is not certain whether he borrowed them or stole them, but if they *were* stolen, the Phoenician horse-traders deserved it.

Furthermore, after the Greeks had been using the letters for a while, the Etruscans of northern Italy appropriated them, and then the Romans, as unoriginal as ever, took them from the Etruscans.

When one considers that the letters had been traveling about from one nation to another for so many hundreds of years, it is amazing that they have remained in such good condition. The only new ones we have are J, U, and W. The Romans did not need them at first, so they came later, as did spaghetti (which they stole from the Chinese) and white clam sauce (which they created themselves, with divine inspiration, of course).

In Appendix XX, a comparative presentation of Phoenician, Greek and Early Latin letter-forms may be found, together with the recipe for white clam sauce, an item of obviously universal interest.

So that the letters may be appreciated to their fullest, the following pages contain a representative sampling, which, it is hoped, will be of some interest to those readers of a curious bent.

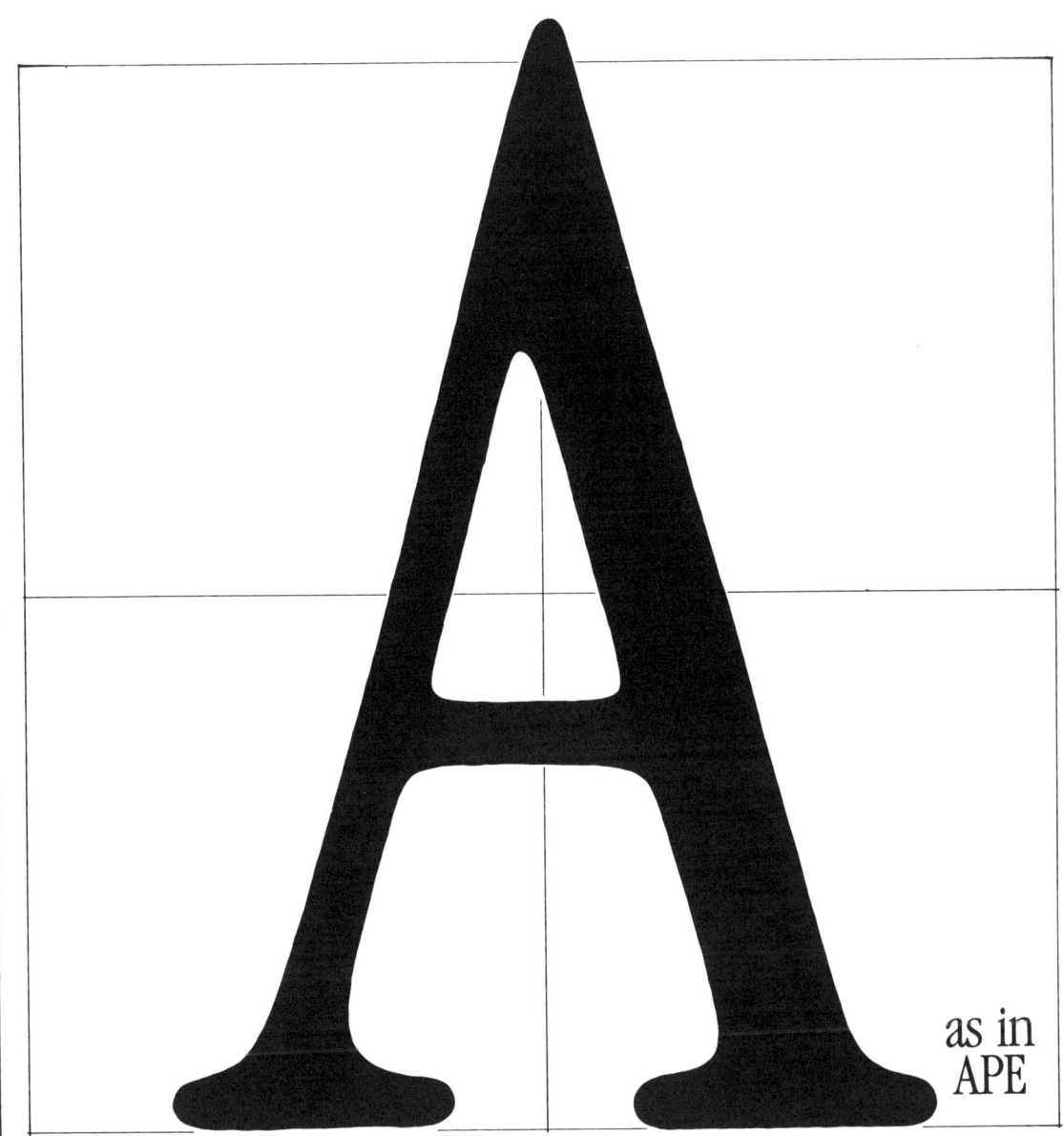
as in
APE

APE

sex ape/peal

ape/partheid

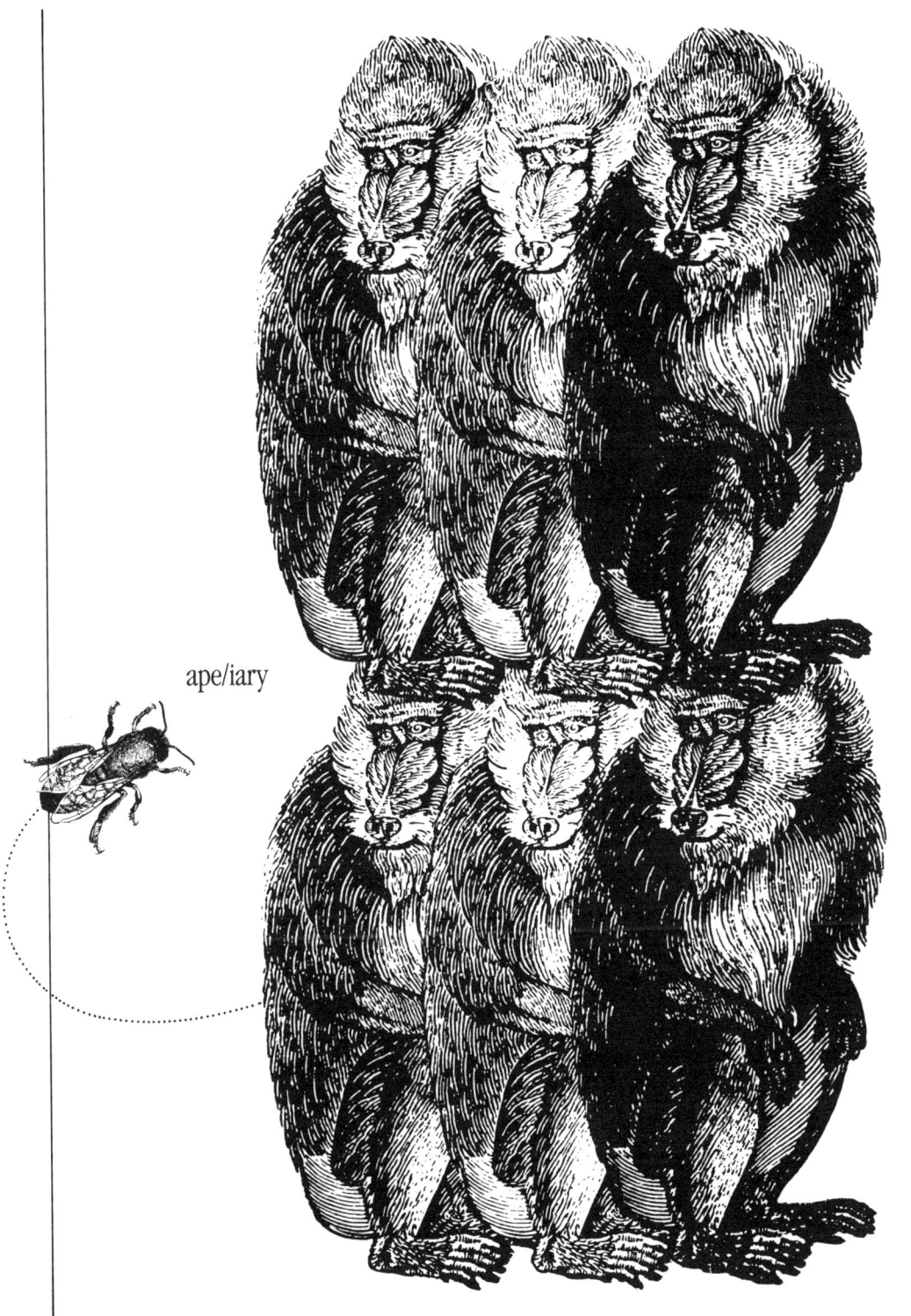

ape/iary

APE

APE

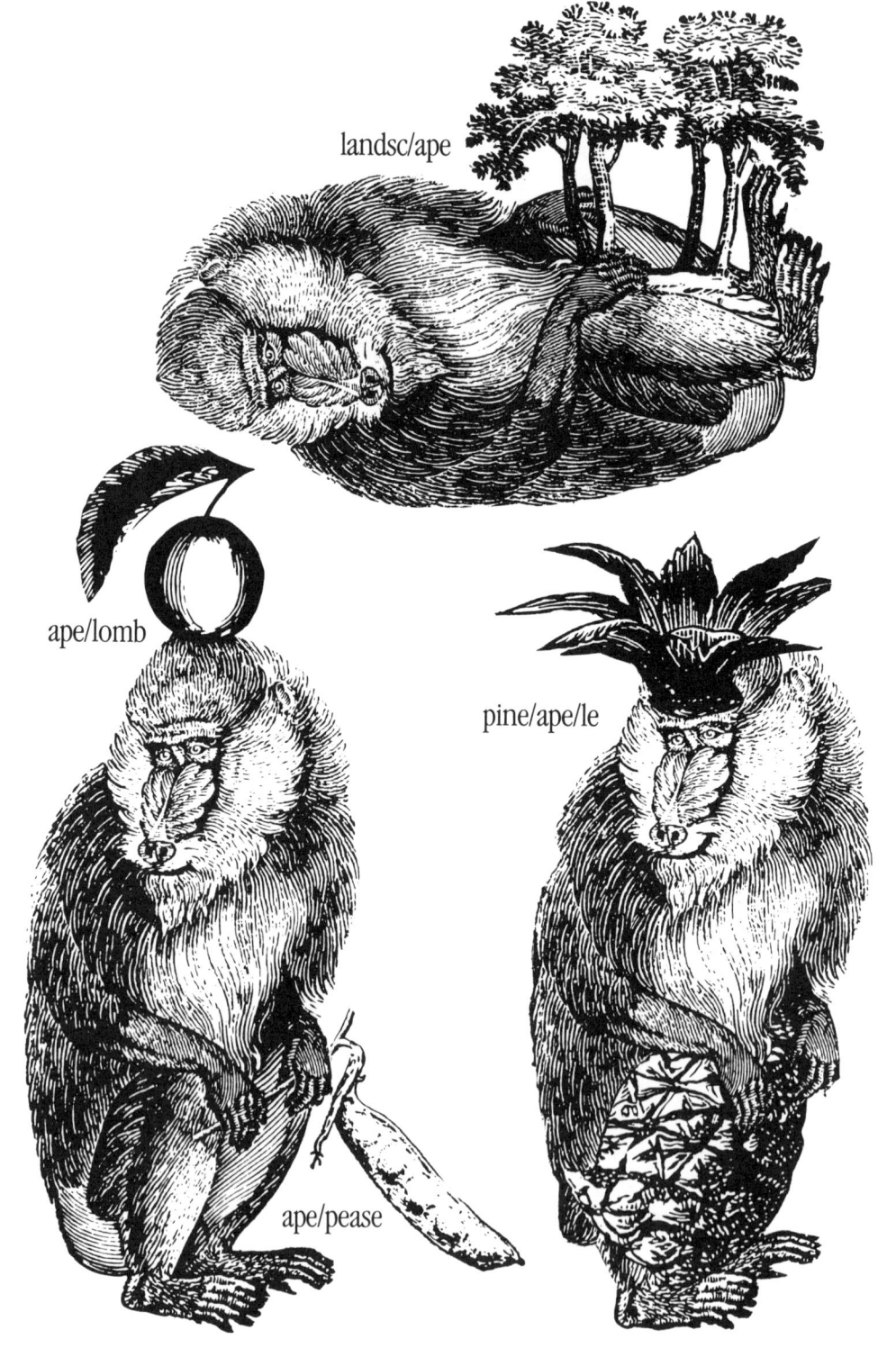

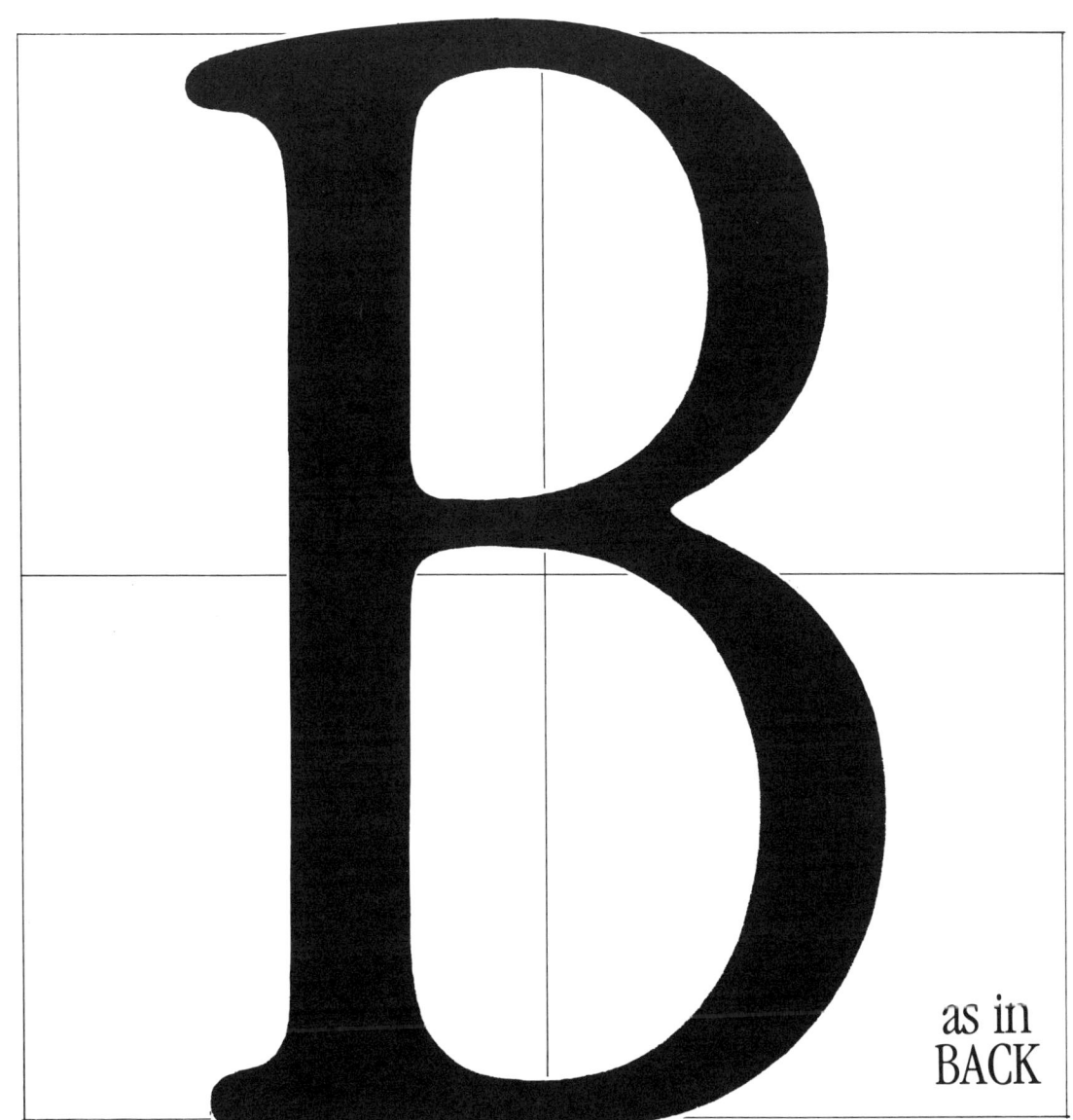

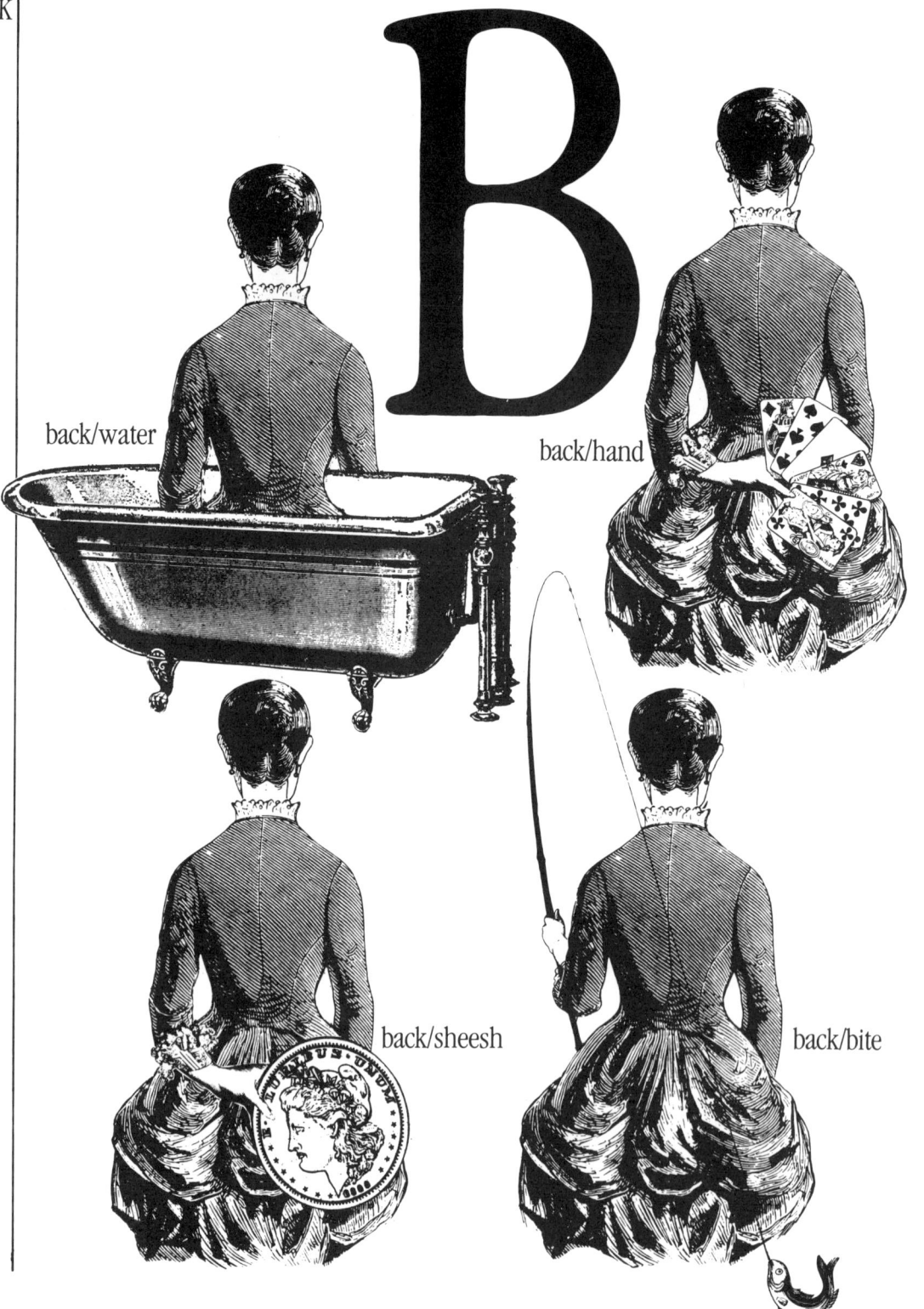

BACK

half/back

back/drop

Johann Sebastian/Back

fin/back   sway/back   back/alaureate

BACK

set/back

back/wash

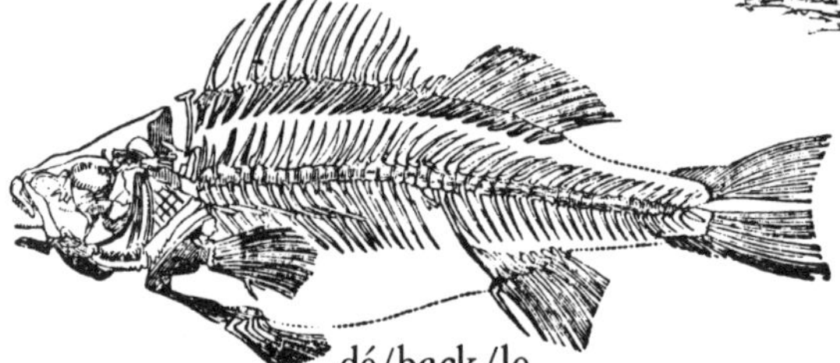

dé/back/le

back/ward

back/down

back/up

back/breaker

bare/back

hump/back

BACK

back/burner

back/biter

taken a/back

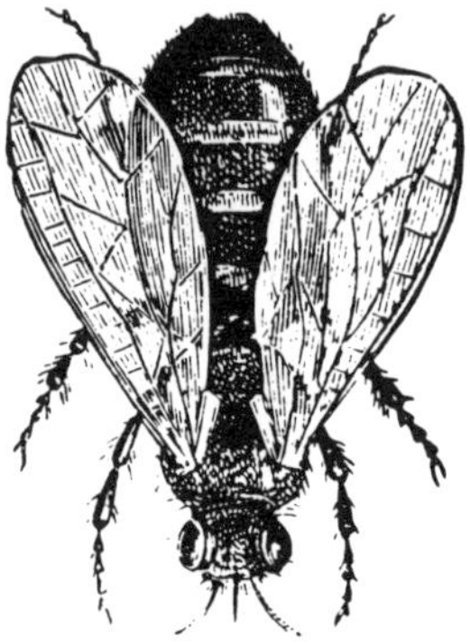

fall/back

back/scratcher

to/back/o

back/side

back/trackers

back/fire

back/analia

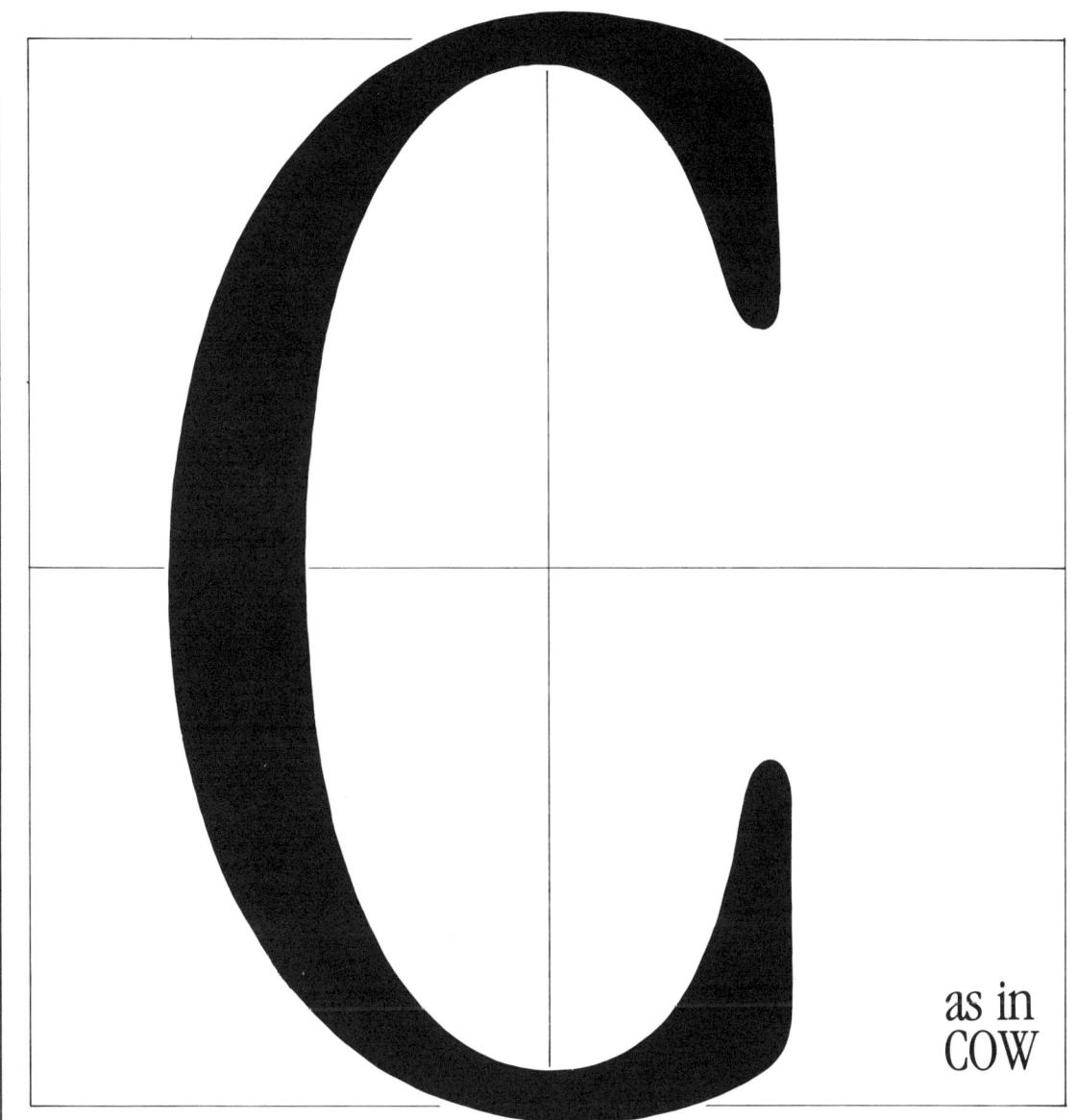

as in
COW

COW

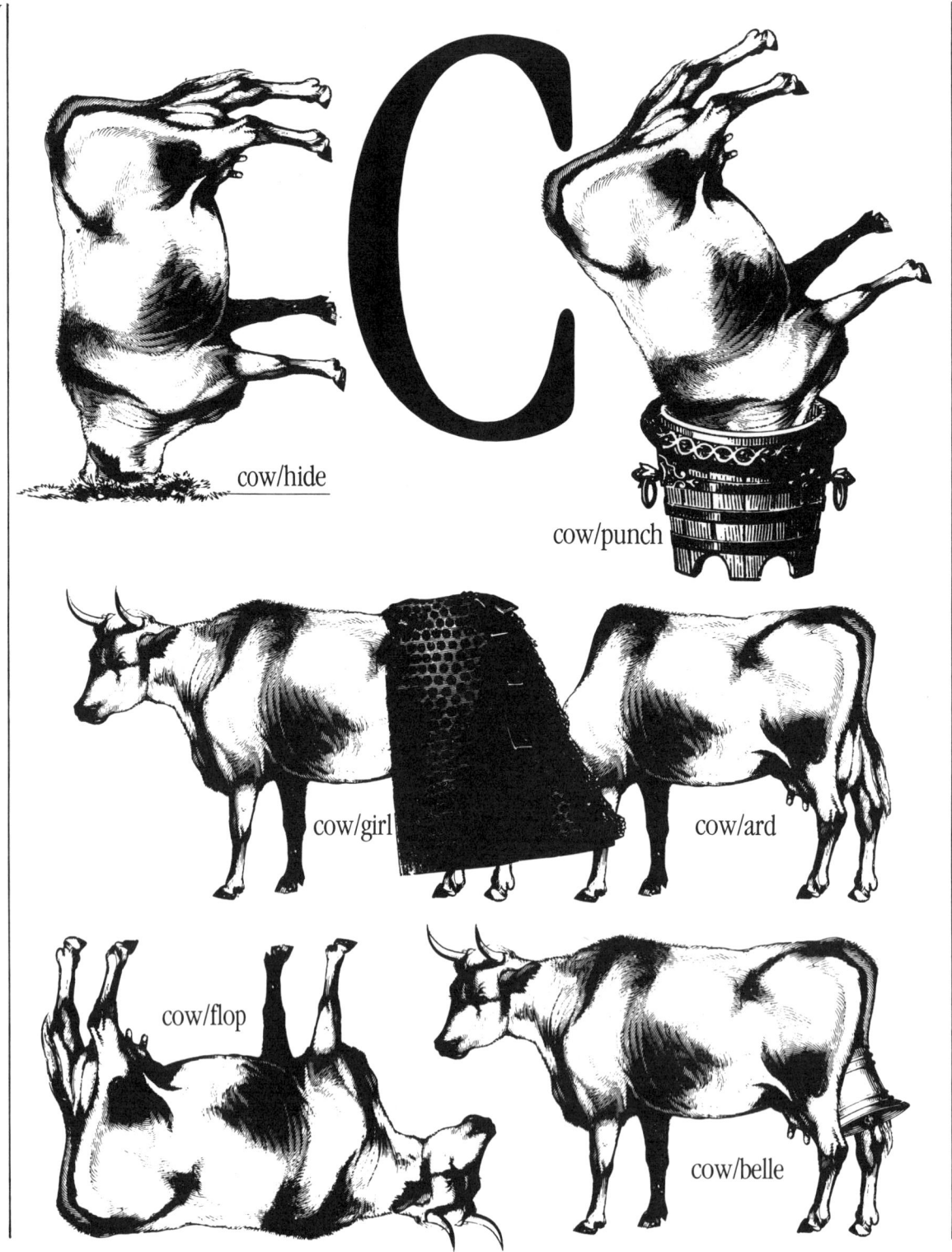

cow/hide
cow/punch
cow/girl
cow/ard
cow/flop
cow/belle

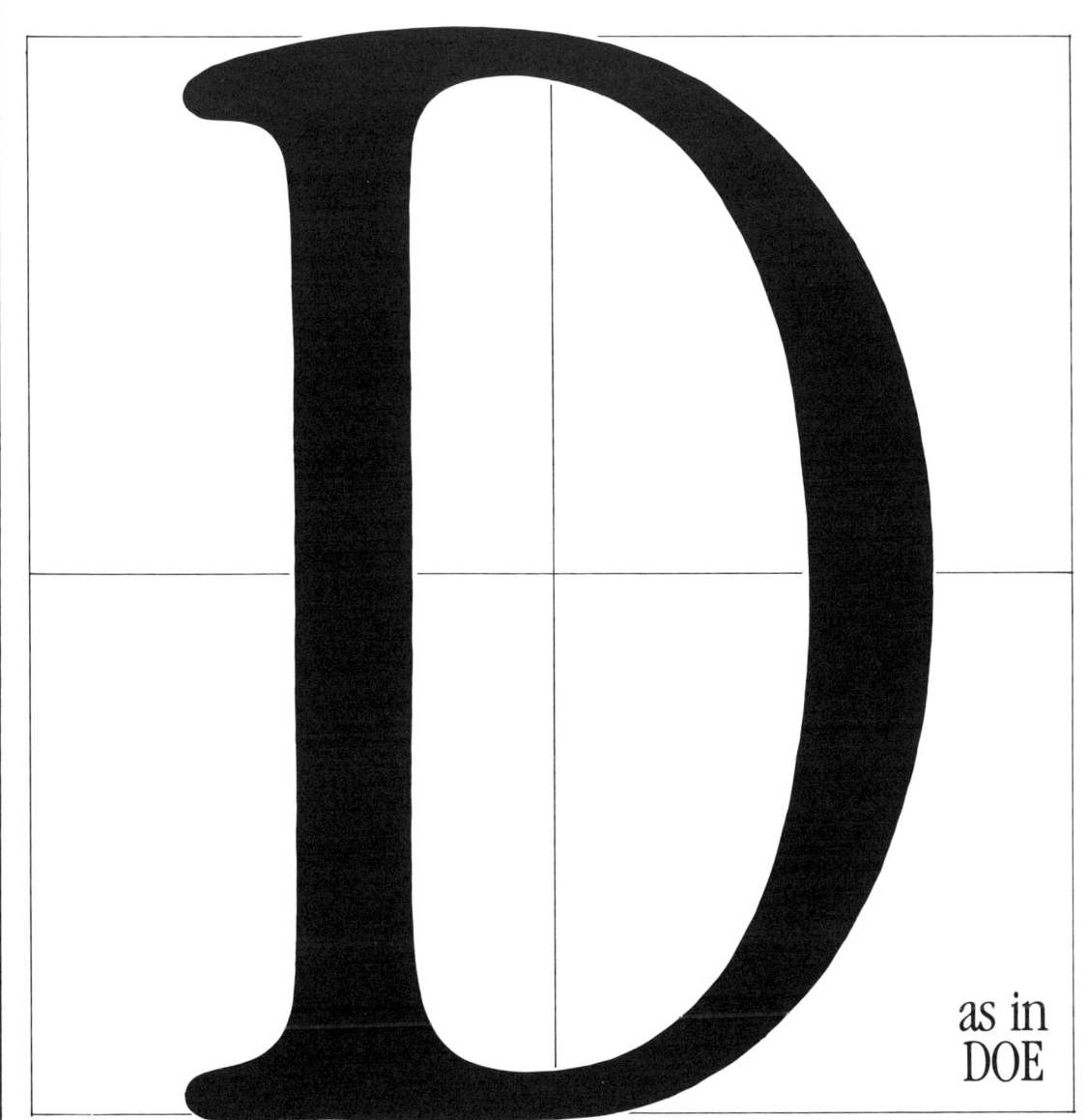

as in
DOE

DOE

mistle/doe

Doe/dalus

doe/berman-pinscher

doe/do

doe/boy

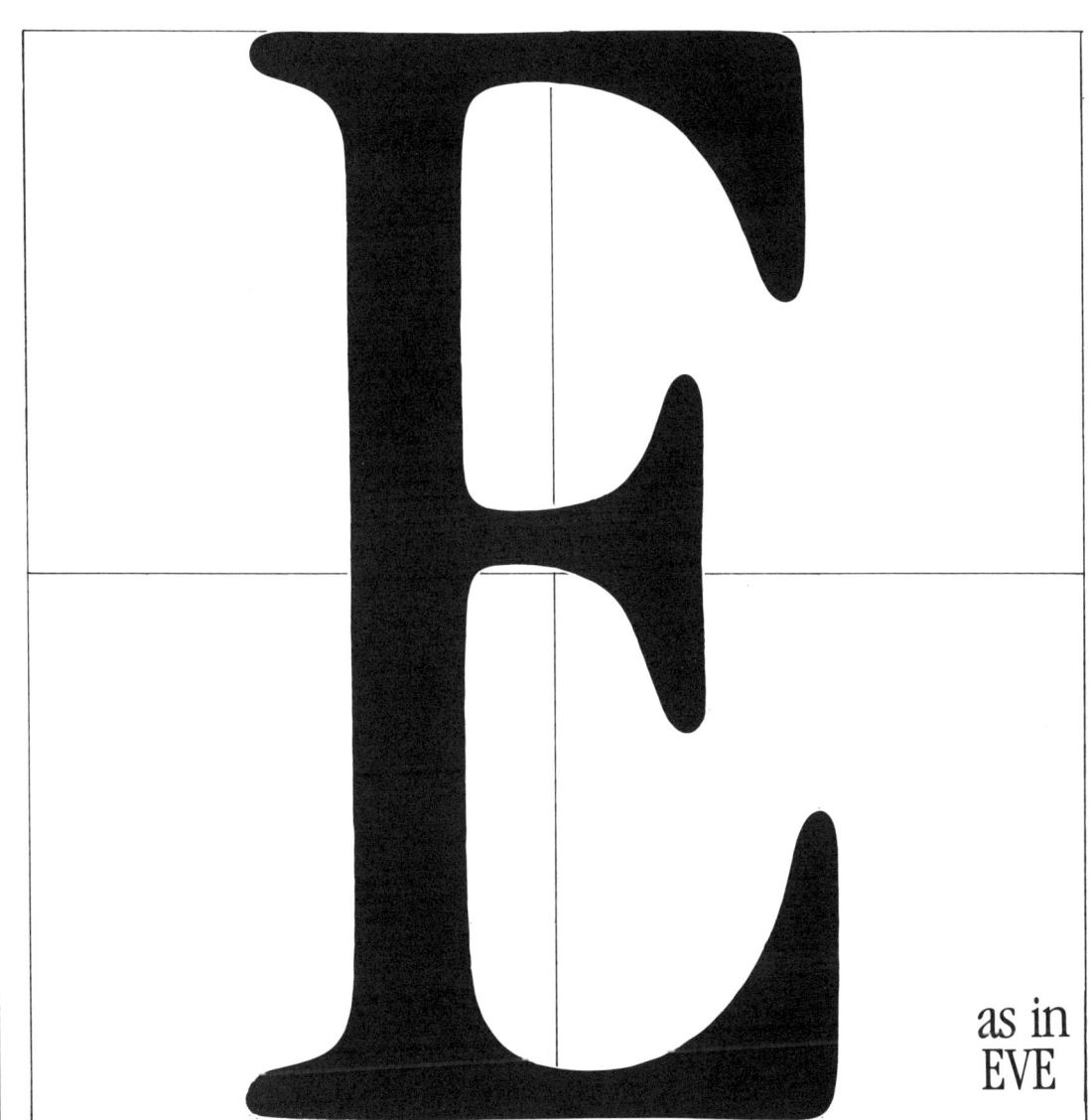

as in
EVE

EVE

E

perc/eve/r

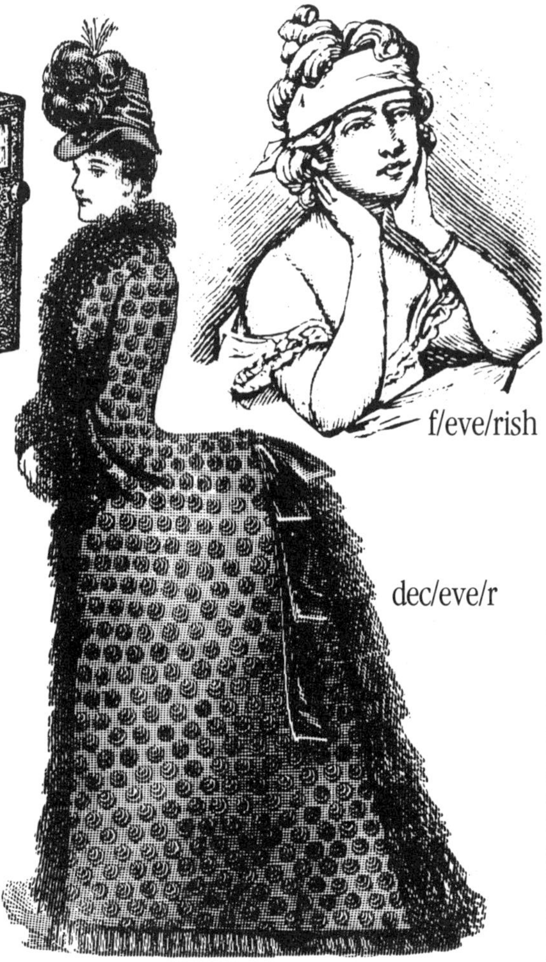

f/eve/rish

dec/eve/r

make-bel/eve

eve/sdropper

Eve/angeline

EVE

b/eve/rage

b/eve/r

ach/eve/r

conc/eve/r

pe/eve/ish

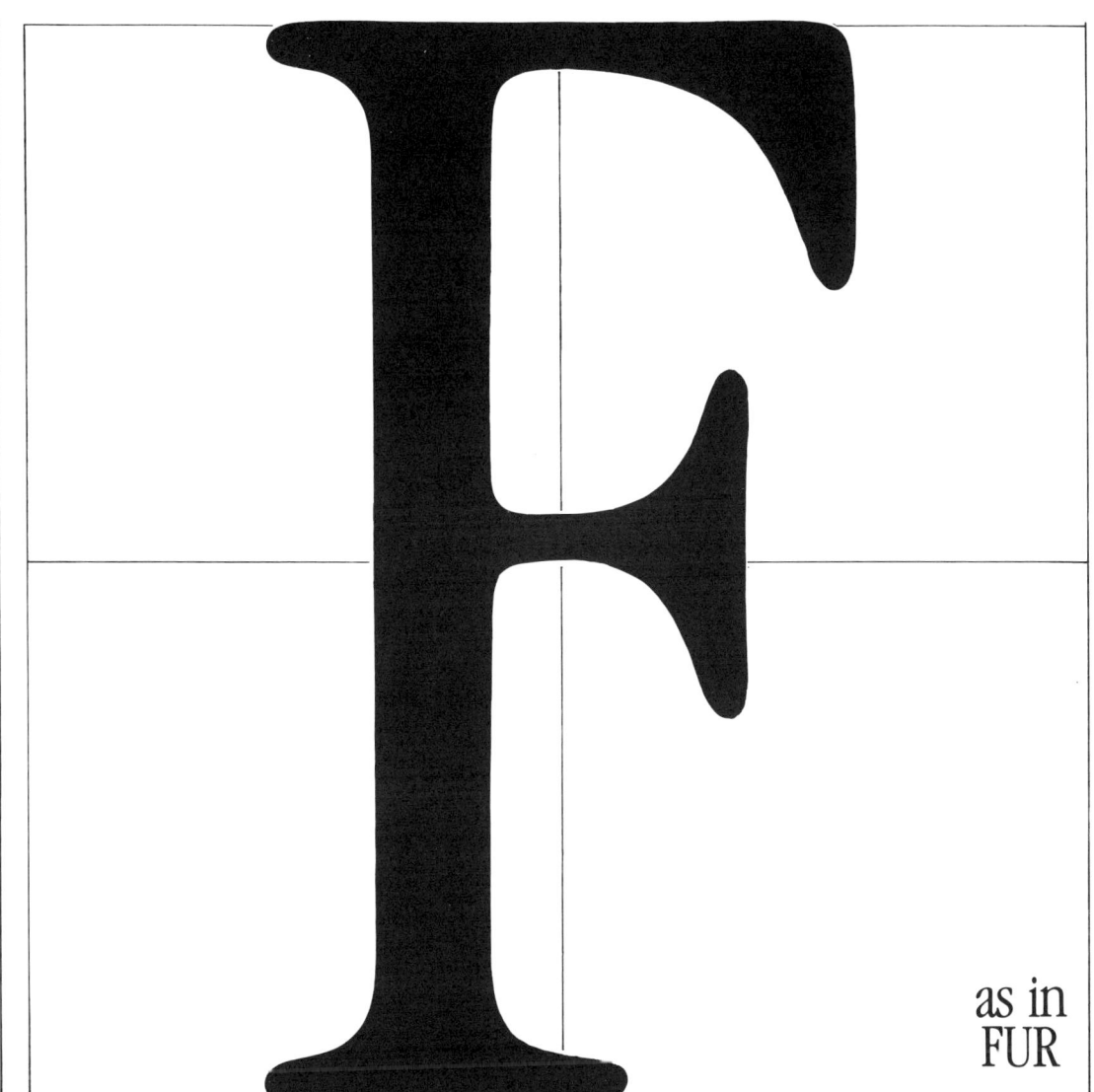

as in
FUR

FUR

fur/tive
fur/mament
de/fur
fur/ager
odori/fur/ous
fur/tility
fur/niture

FUR

FUR

fur/st-aid

fur/lorn

per/fur/mance

fur/father

fur/midable

cy/fur/ing

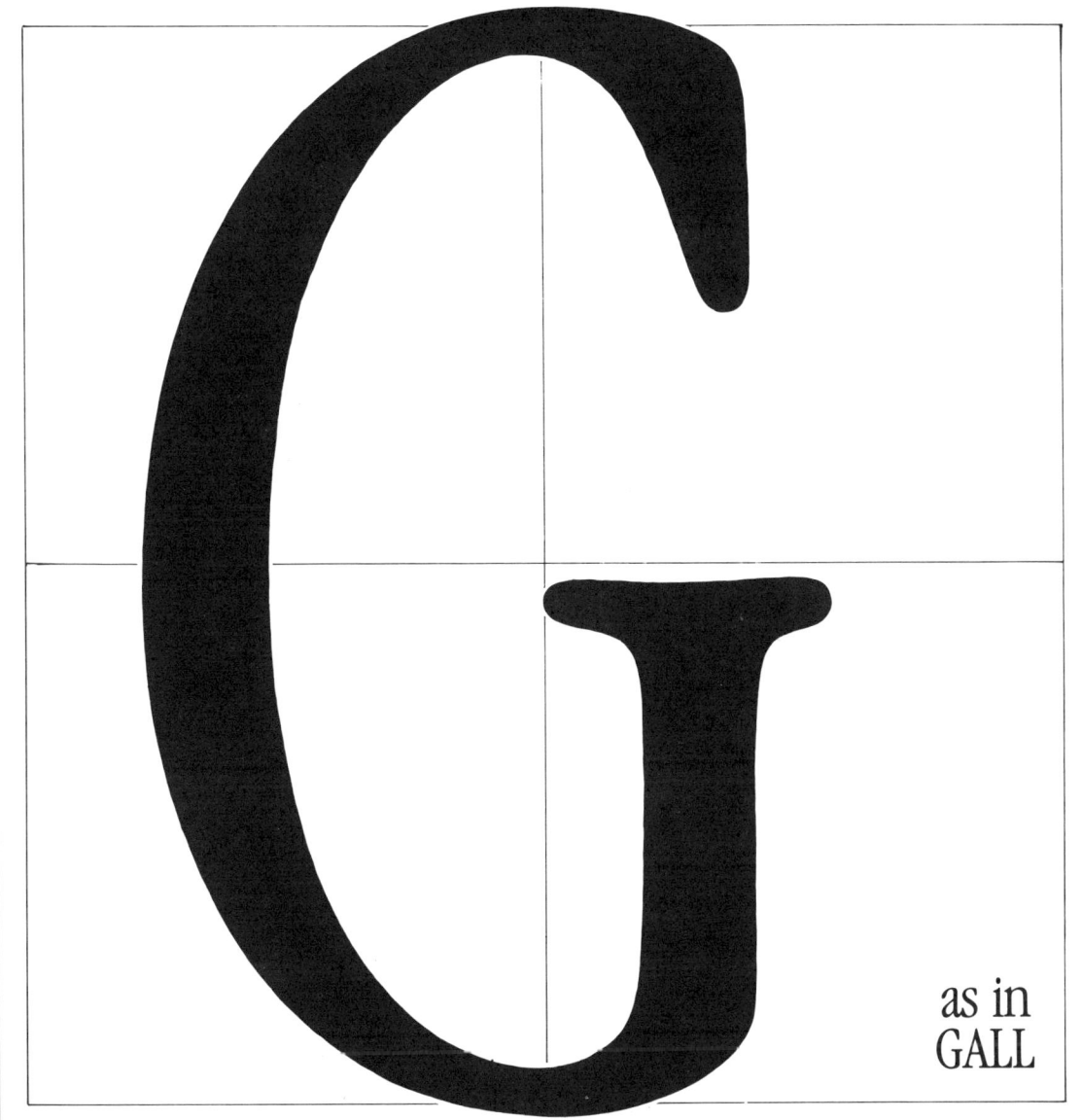

as in
GALL

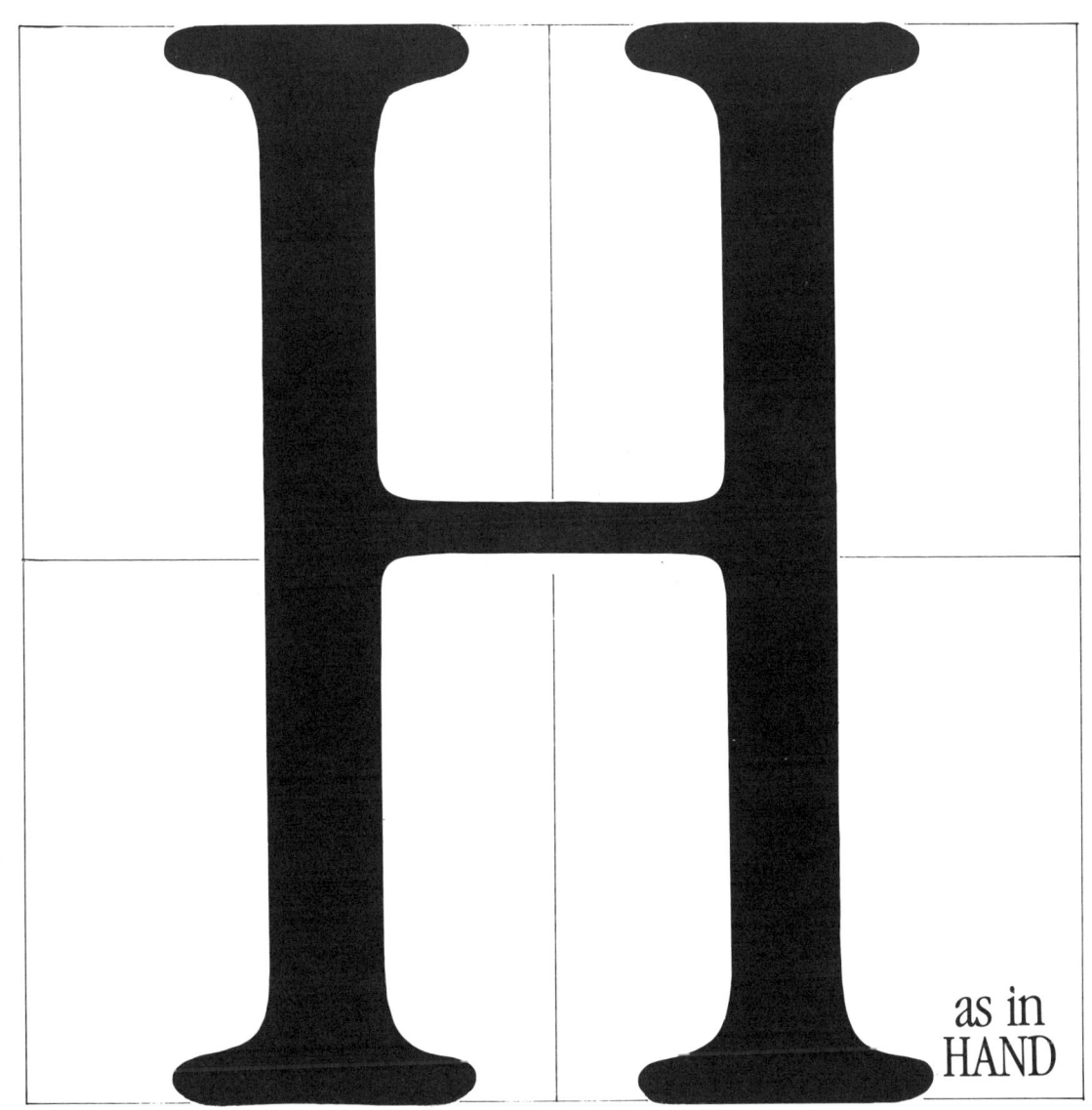
as in HAND

HAND

hand/bag

hand/kerchief

glad/hand

off/hand   hand/cuff   hand/lers

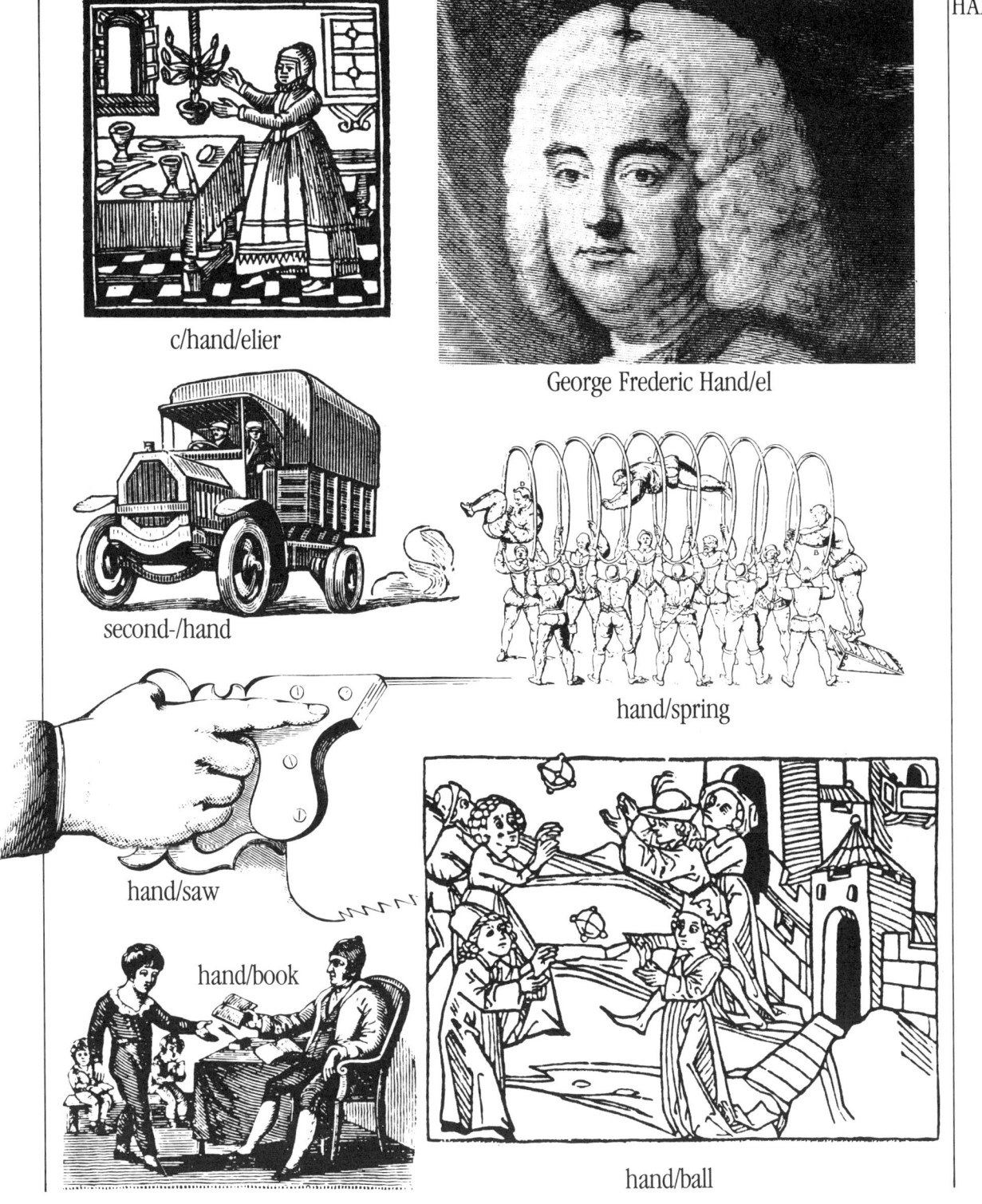

HAND

hand/out

red/hand/ed

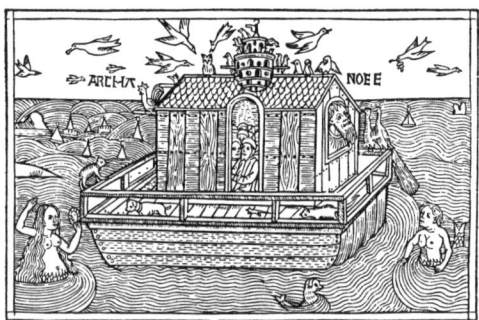
hand/y-man

hand/-to-mouth

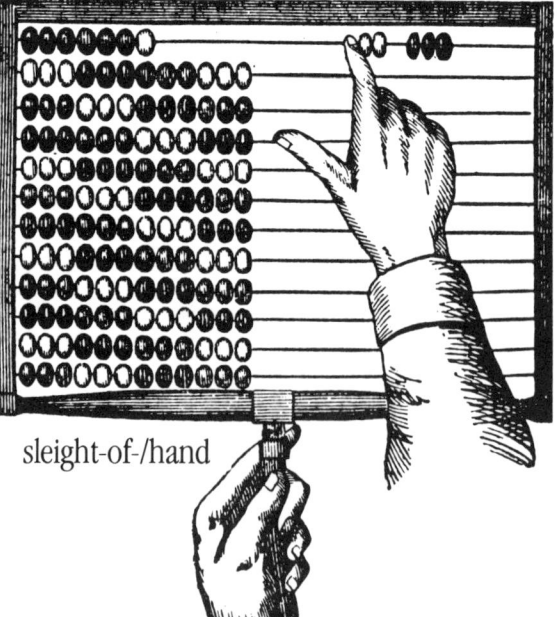
sleight-of-/hand

IMP

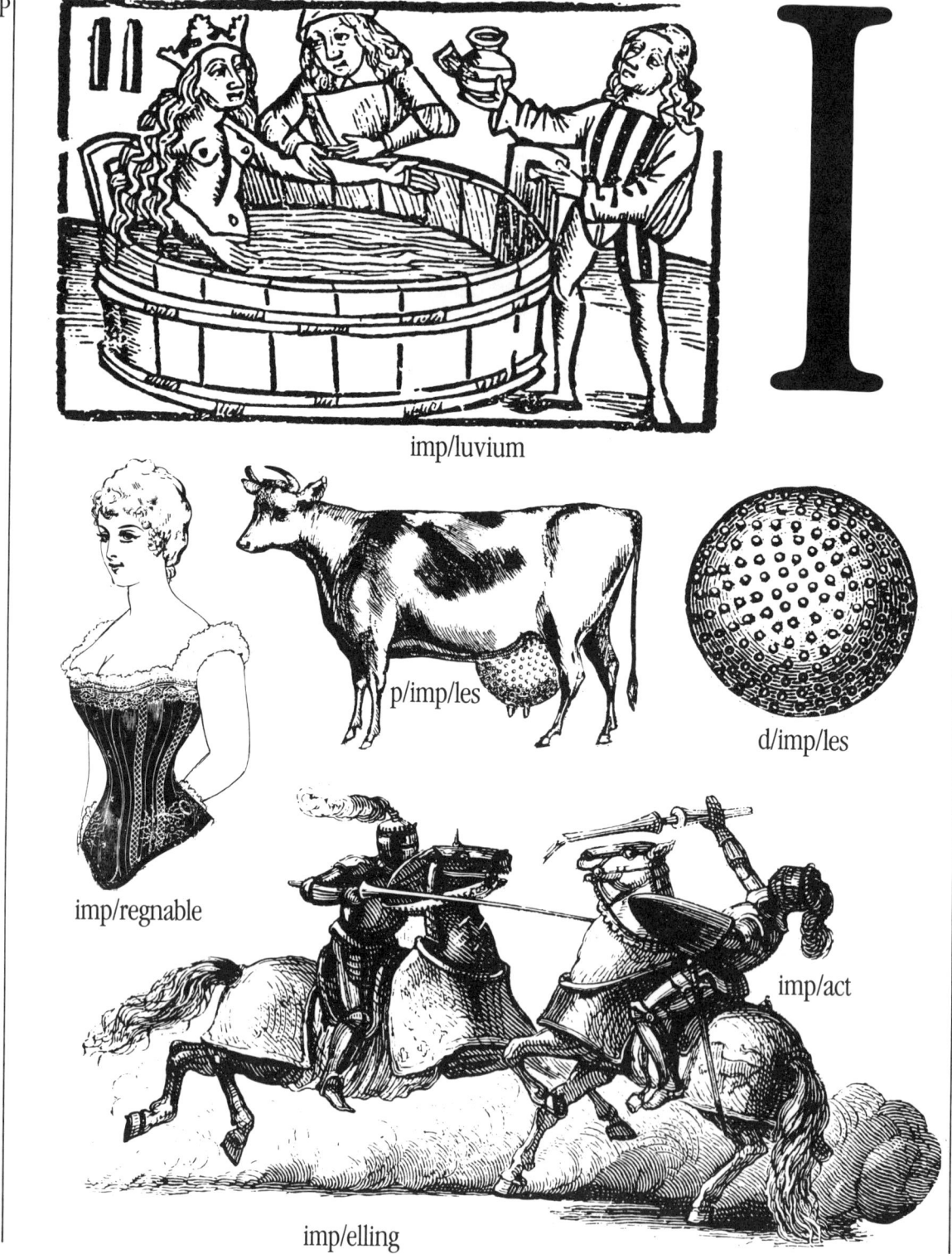

imp/luvium

p/imp/les

d/imp/les

imp/regnable

imp/act

imp/elling

IMP

imp/recation

imp/ropriety

imp/udent

bl/imp

imp/osing

l/imp

as in
JUG

JUG

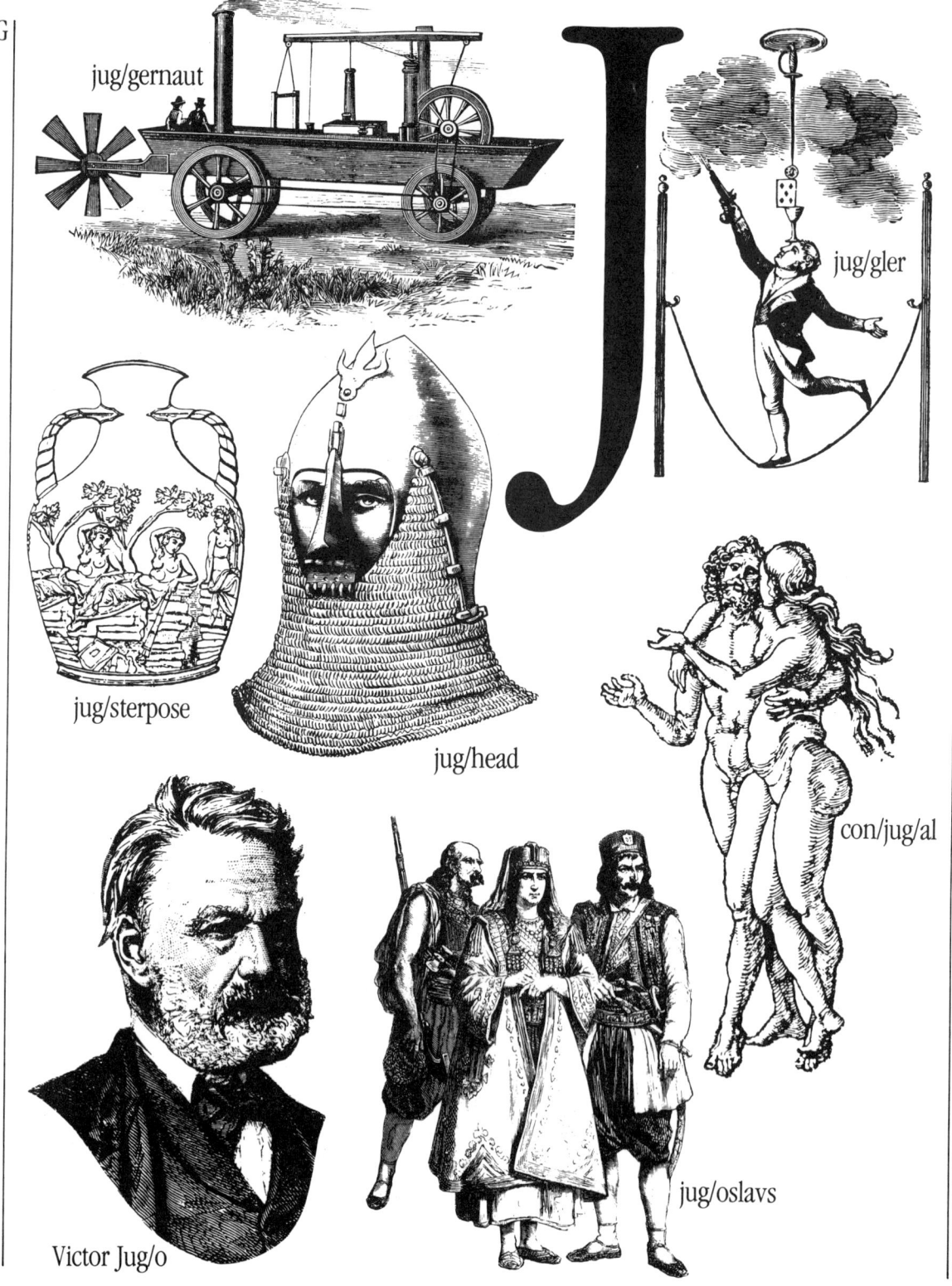

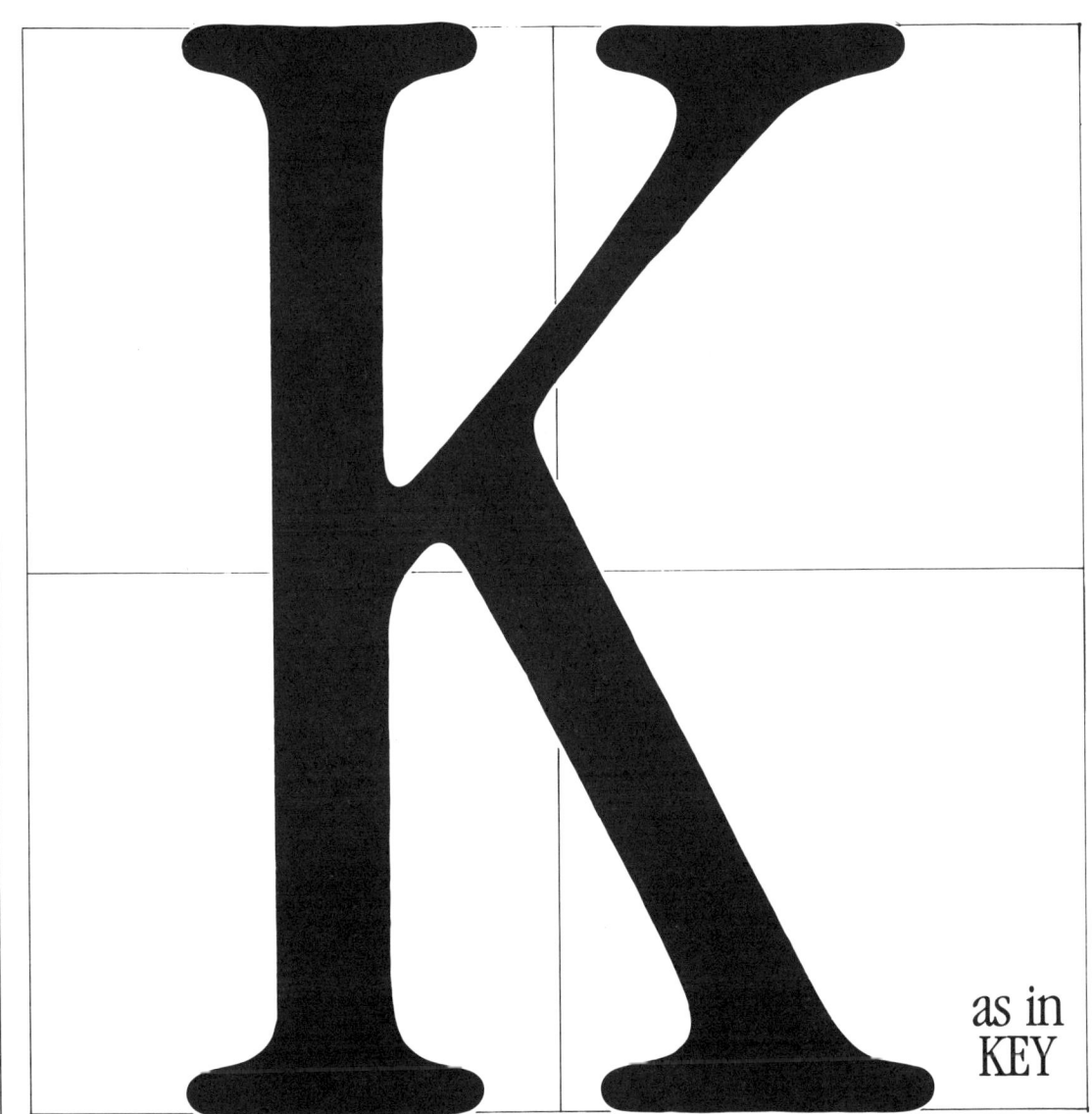

as in
KEY

KEY

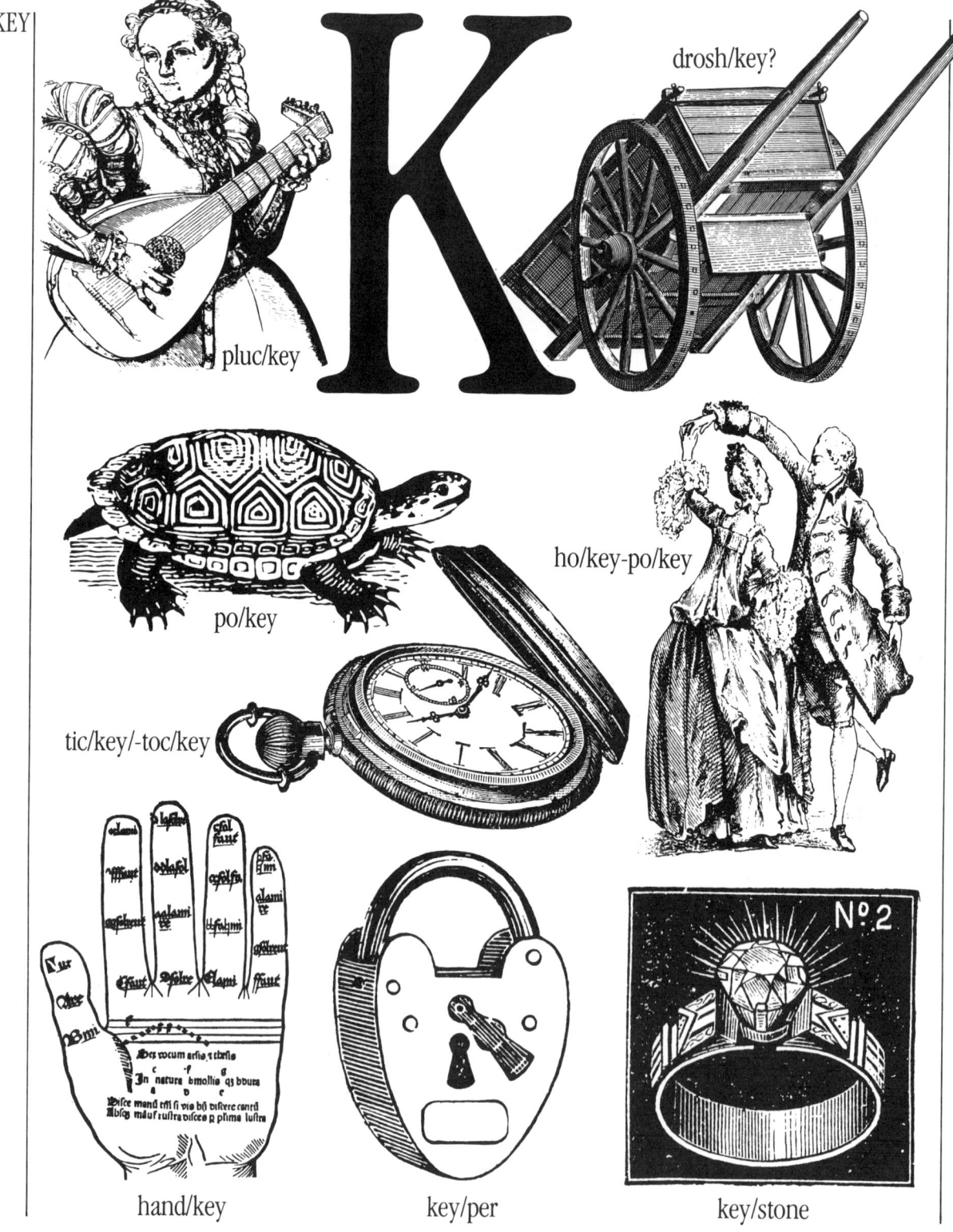

pluc/key
drosh/key?
po/key
ho/key-po/key
tic/key/-toc/key
hand/key
key/per
key/stone

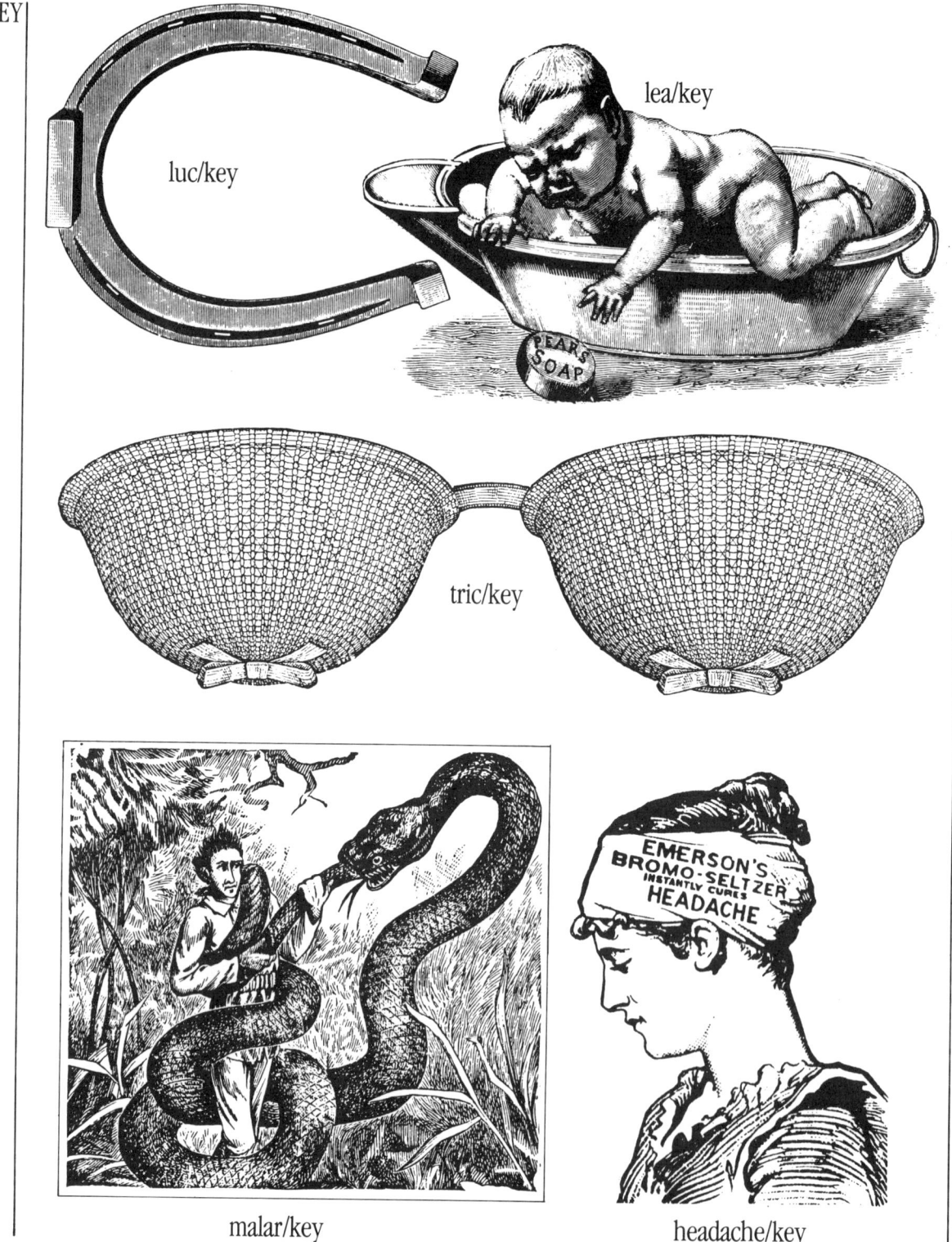

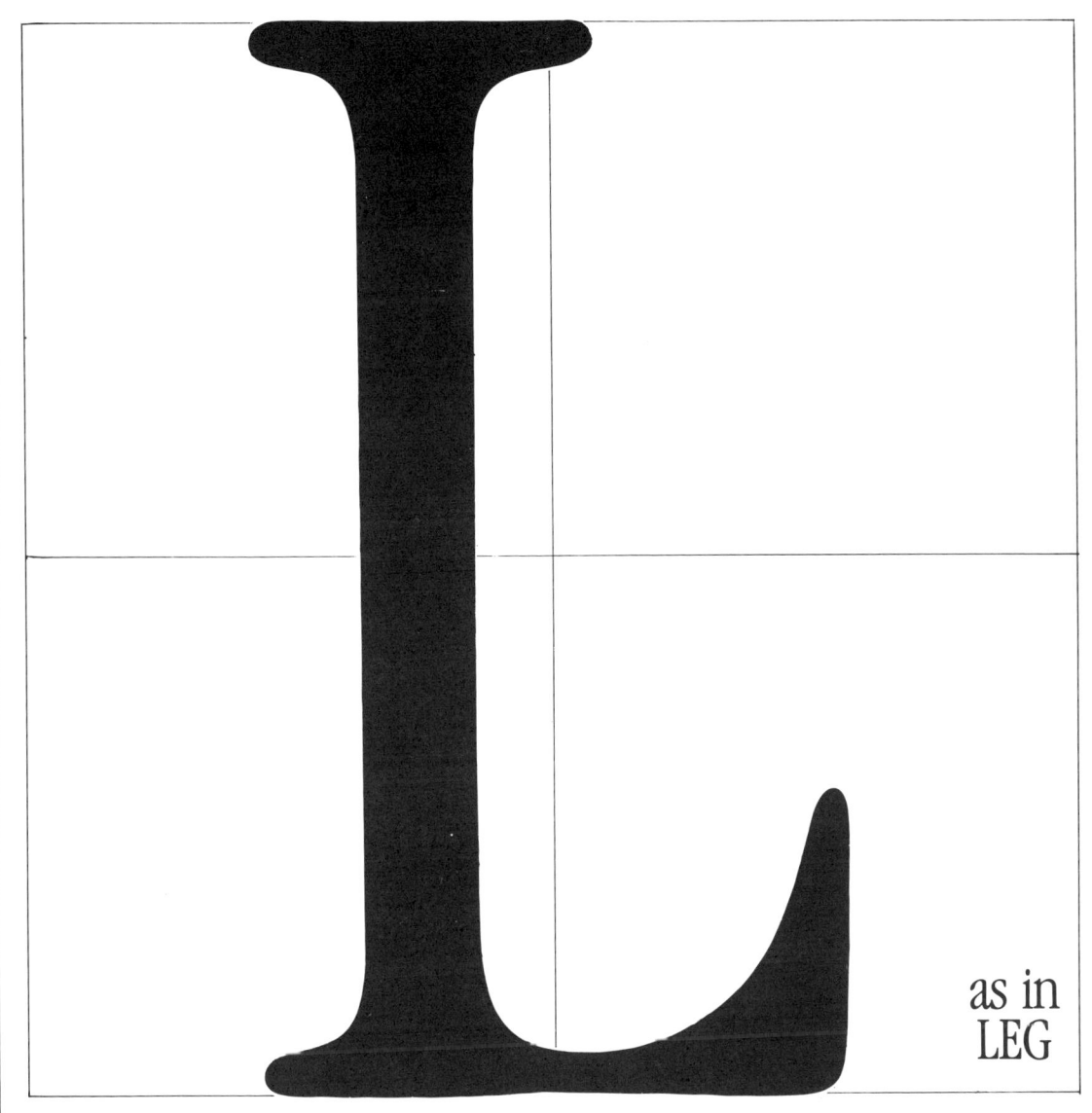

as in
LEG

LEG

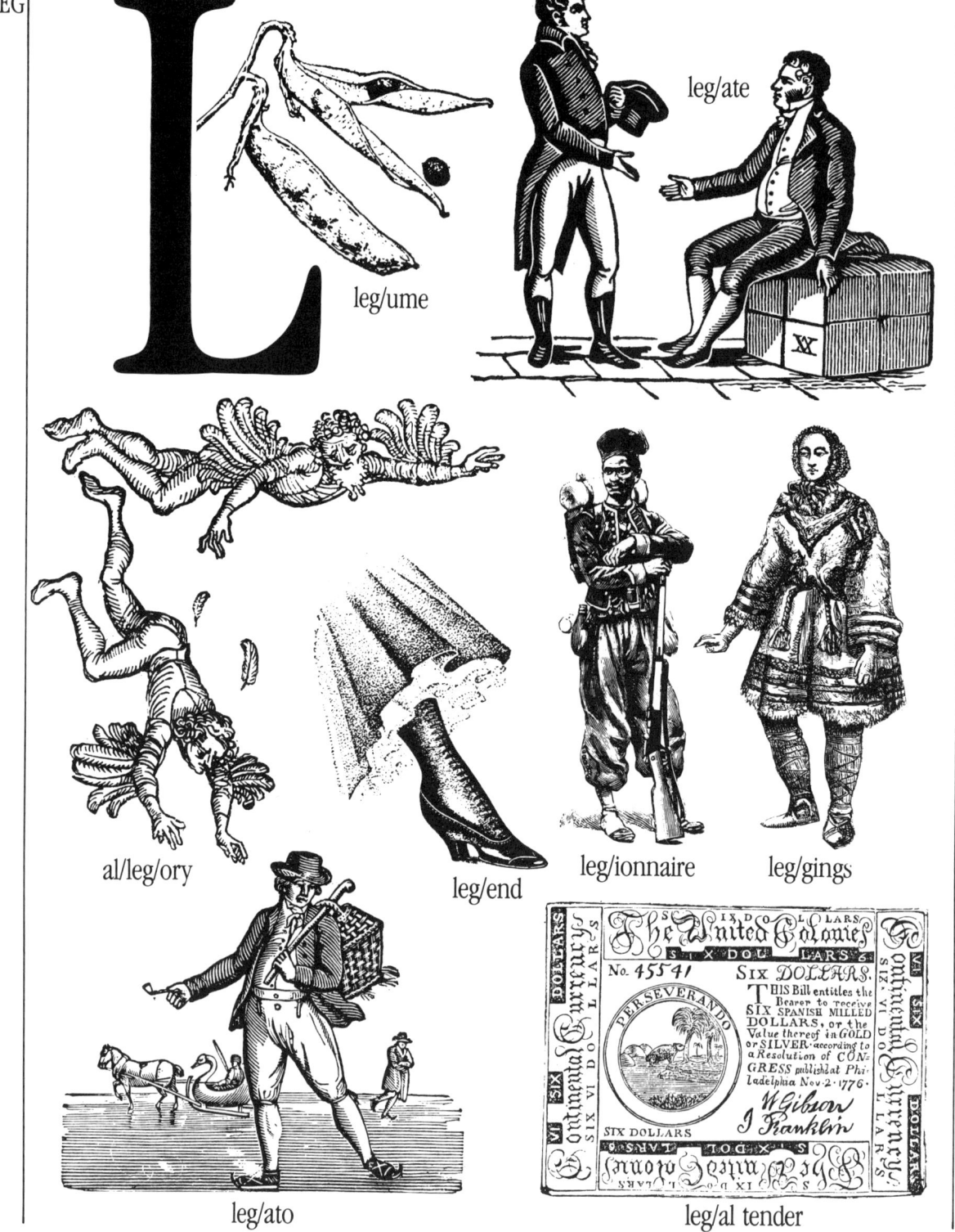

leg/ume

leg/ate

al/leg/ory

leg/end

leg/ionnaire

leg/gings

leg/ato

leg/al tender

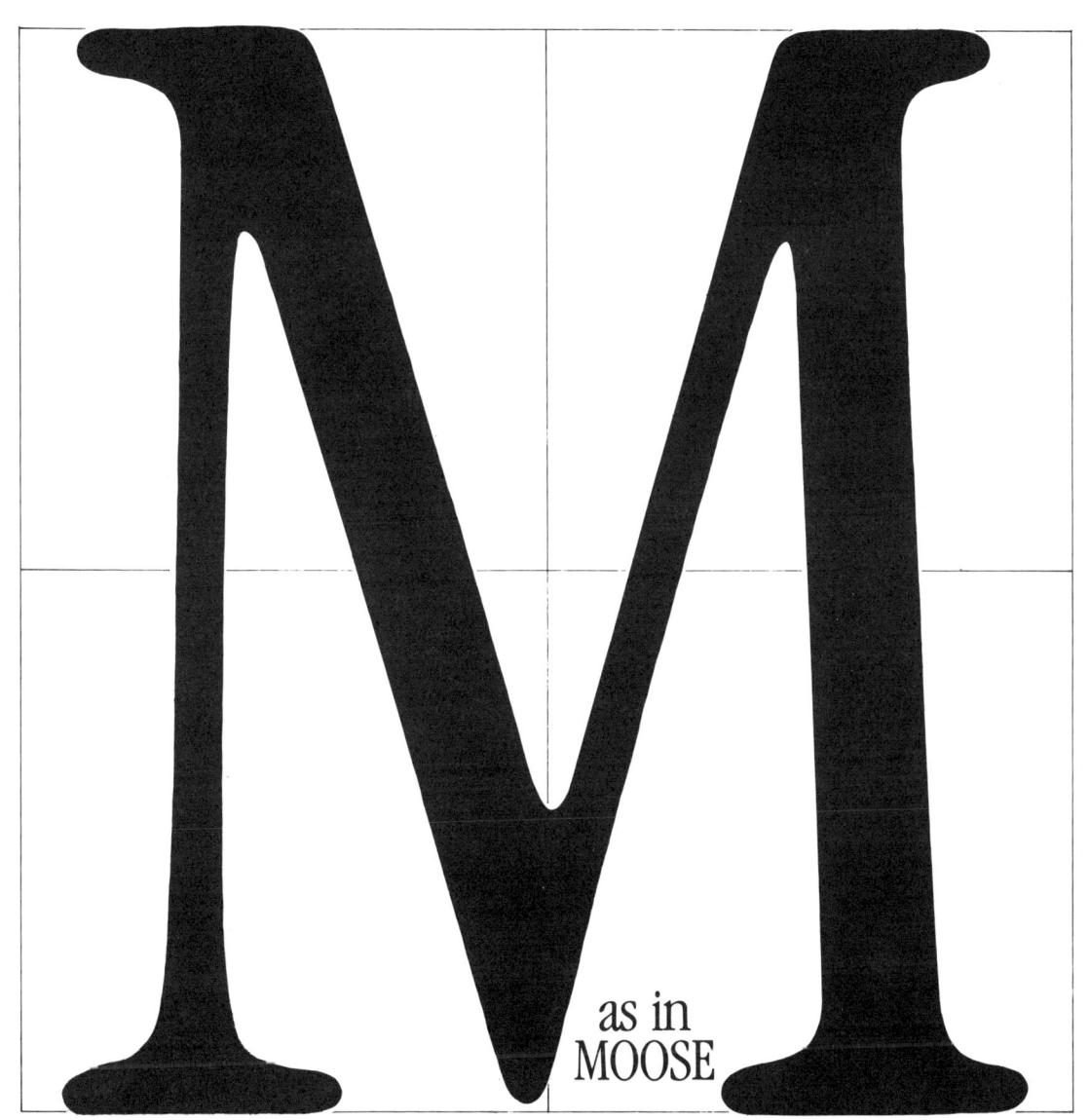

as in
MOOSE

MOOSE

moose/oleum

"Mickey"/moose

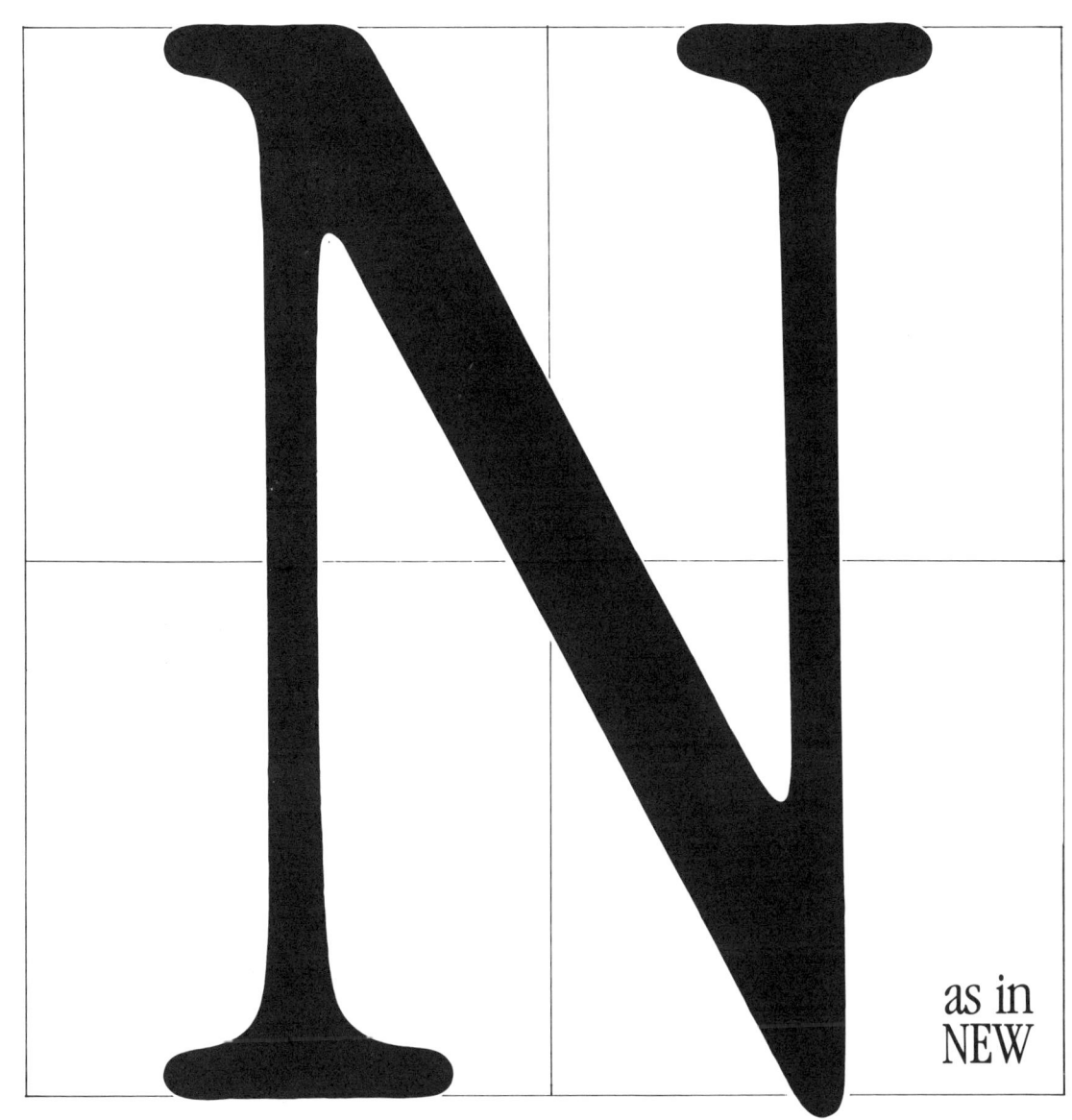
as in
NEW

NEW

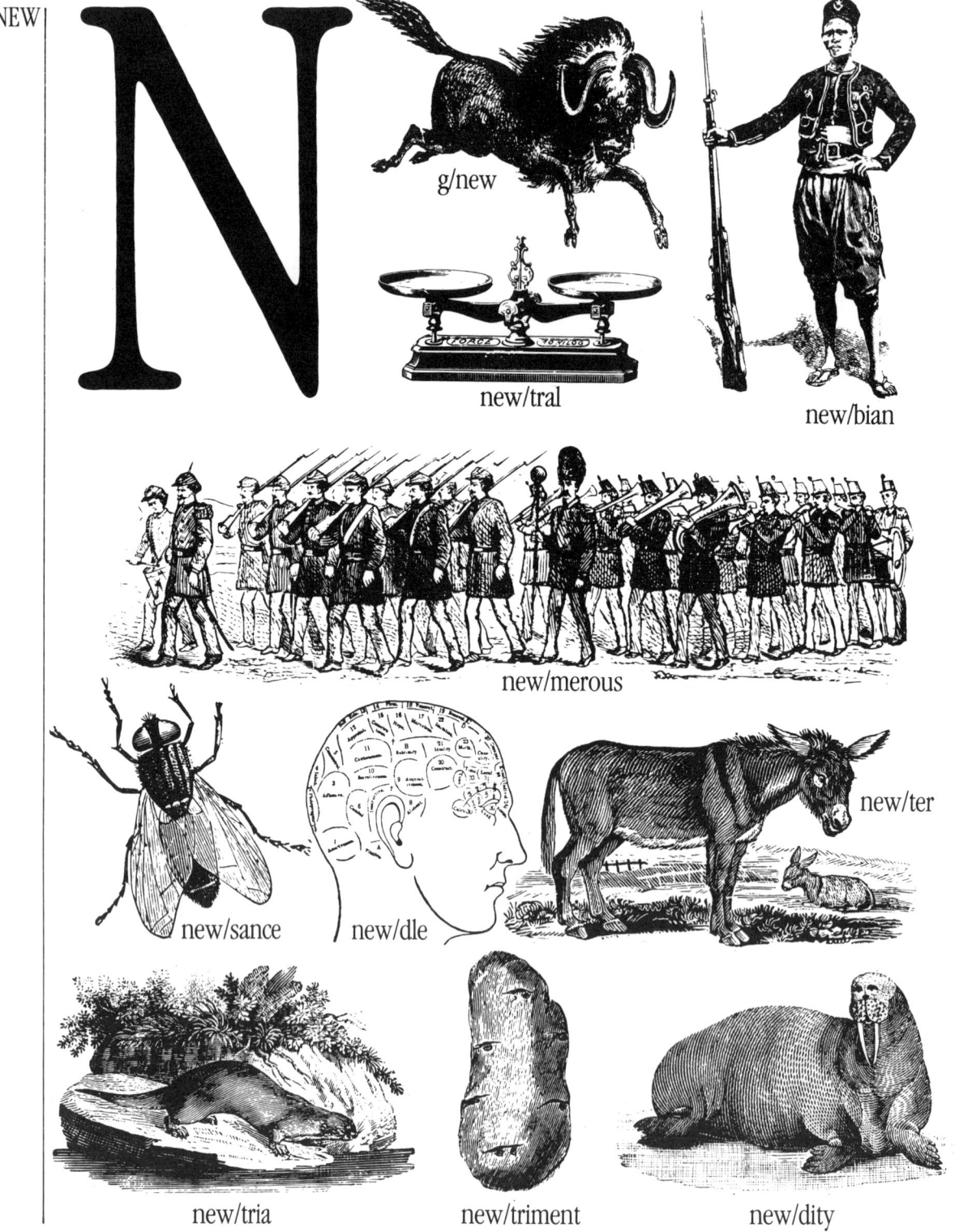

g/new

new/tral

new/bian

new/merous

new/sance

new/dle

new/ter

new/tria

new/triment

new/dity

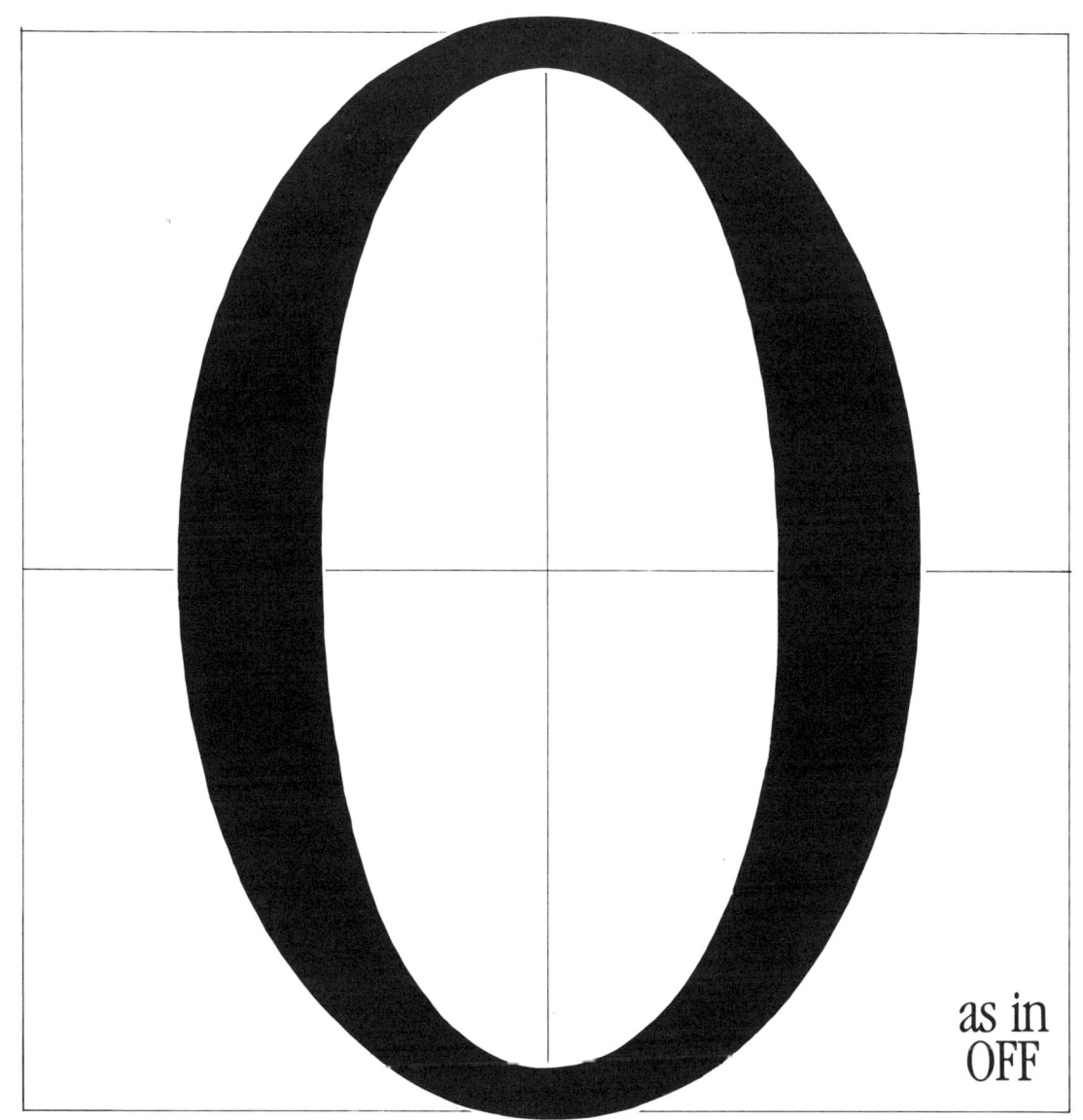

as in
OFF

OFF

O

off/ering

off/shoot

off/shore

stand/off/-ish

d/off

off/icer

off/spring

t/off

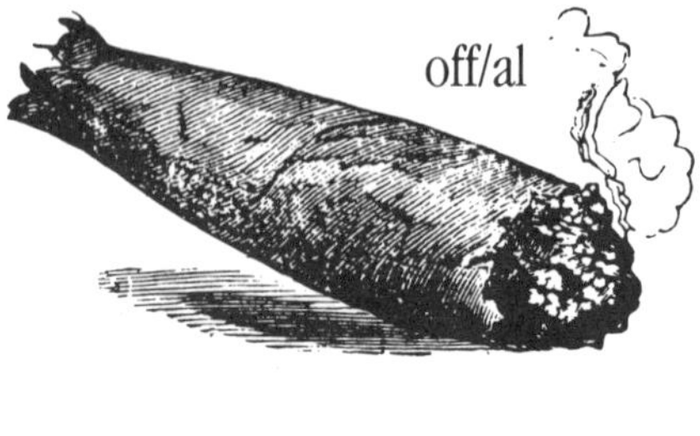

off/al

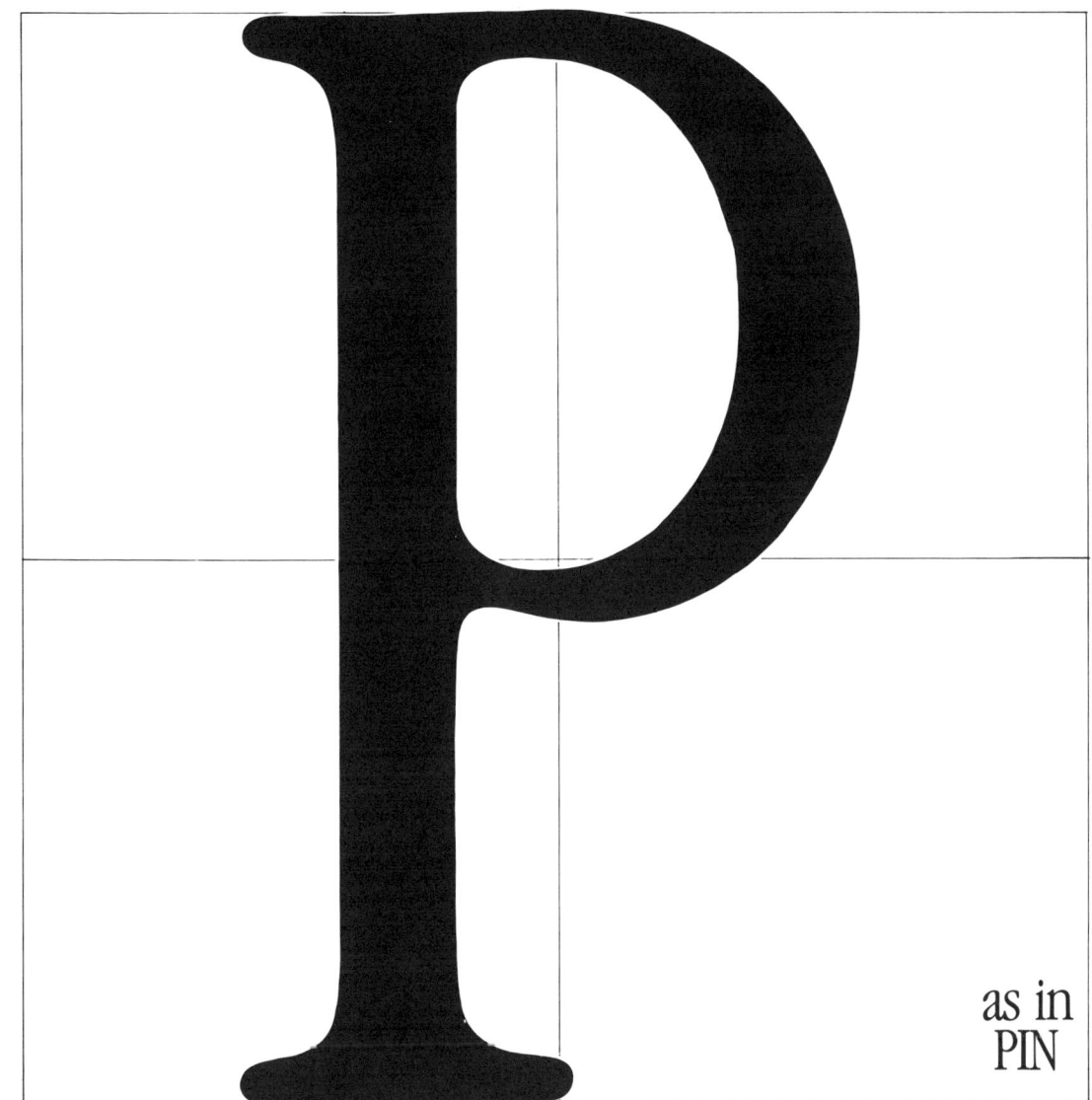

as in
PIN

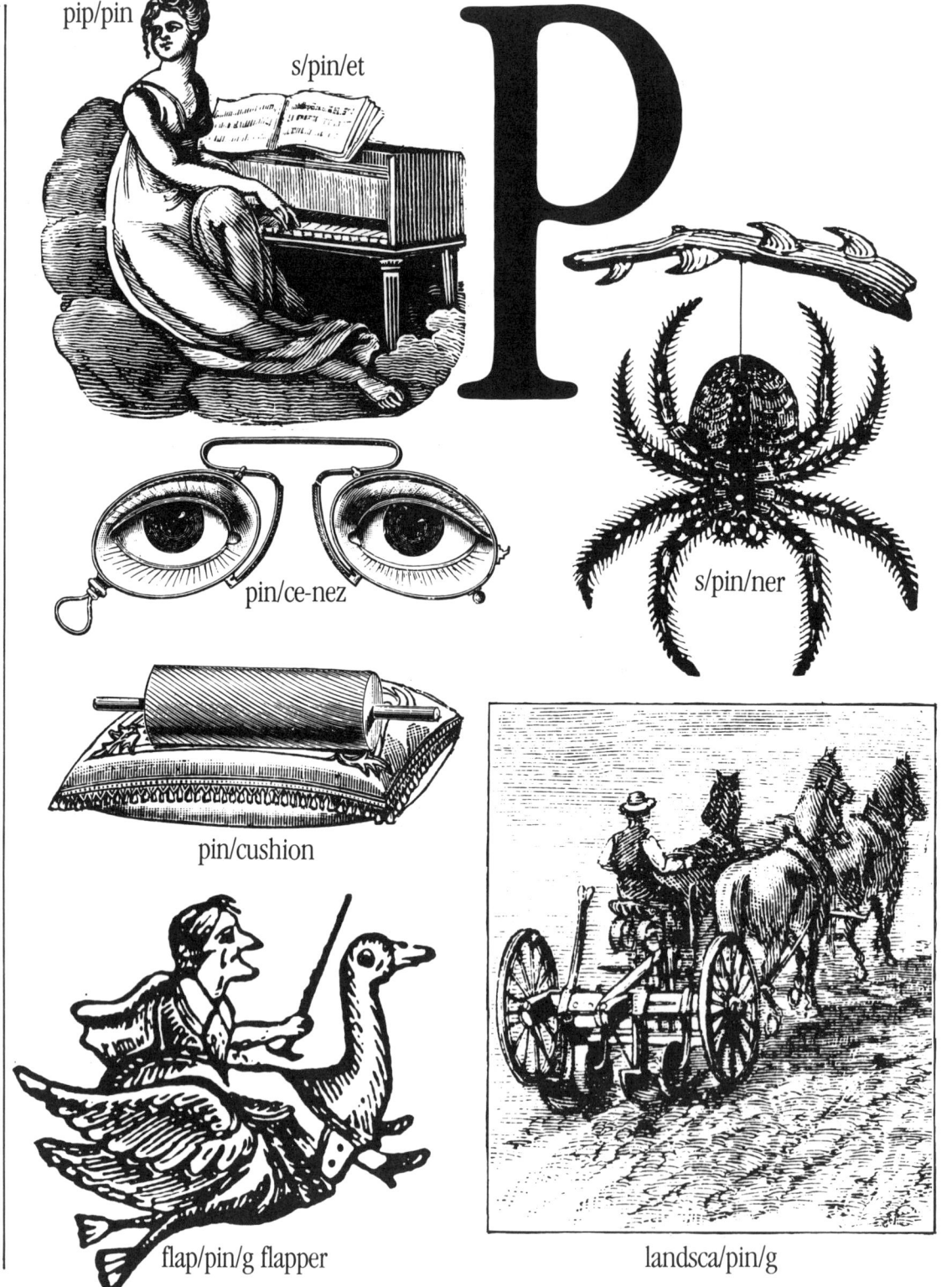

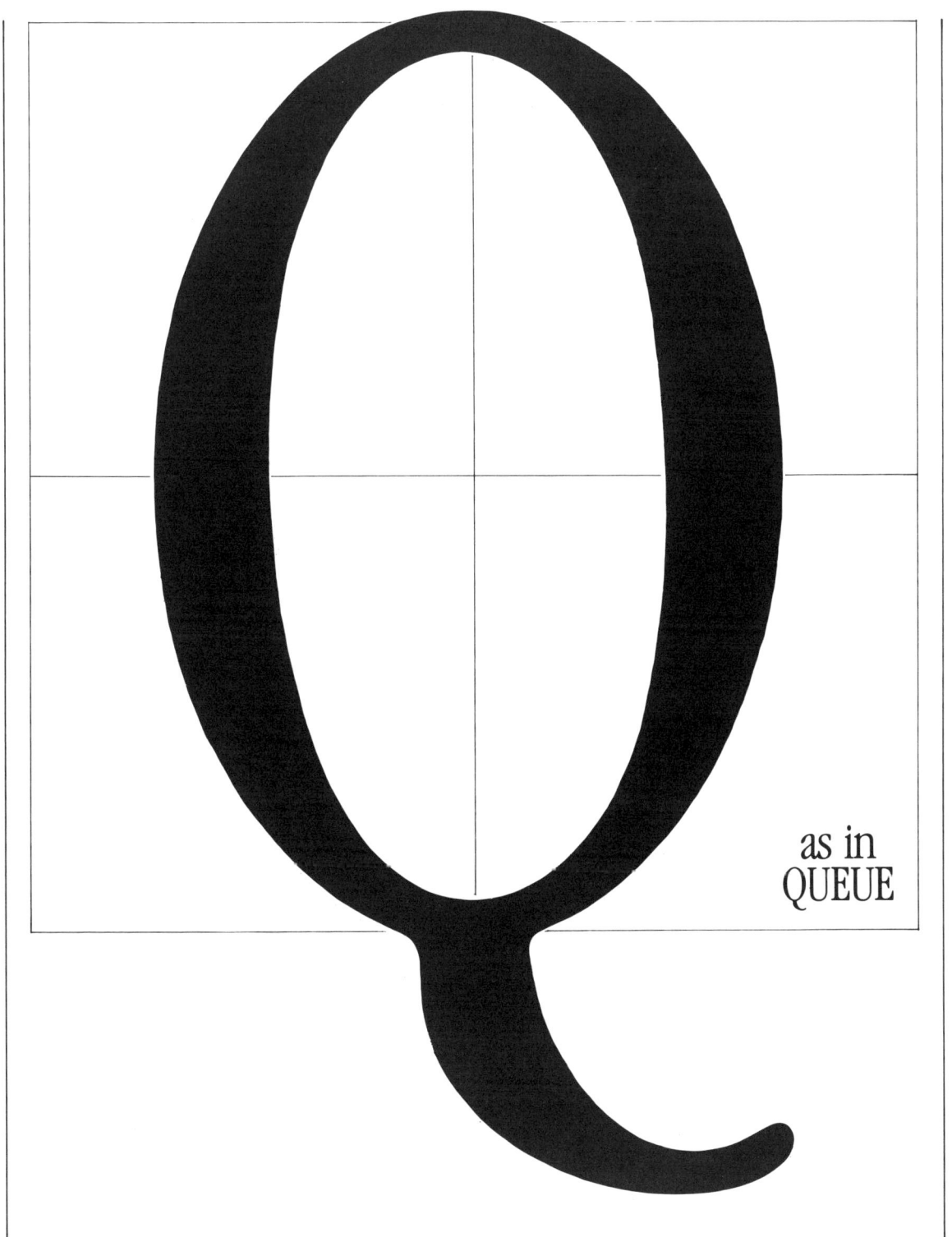

as in
QUEUE

QUEUE

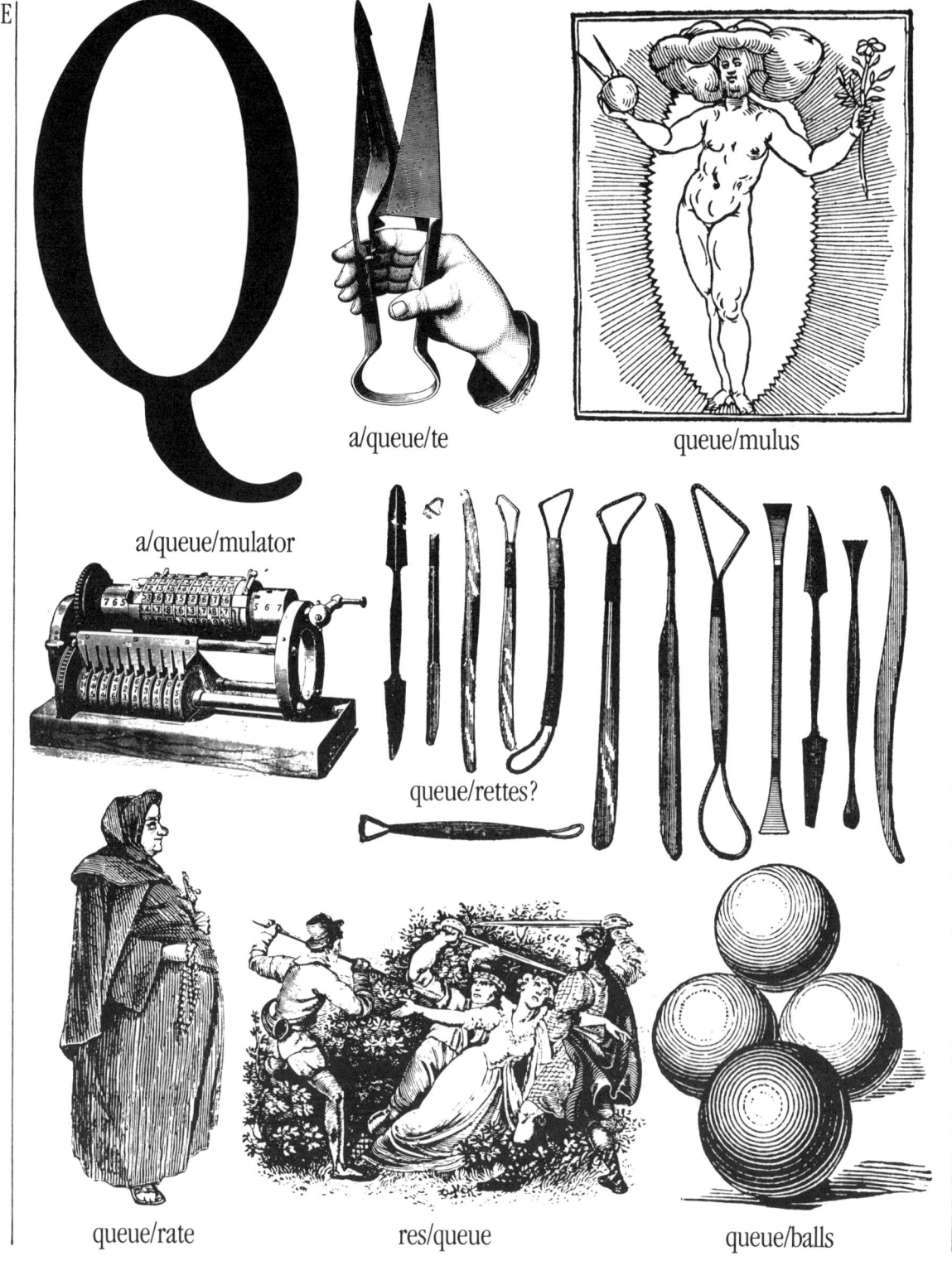

a/queue/te

queue/mulus

a/queue/mulator

queue/rettes?

queue/rate

res/queue

queue/balls

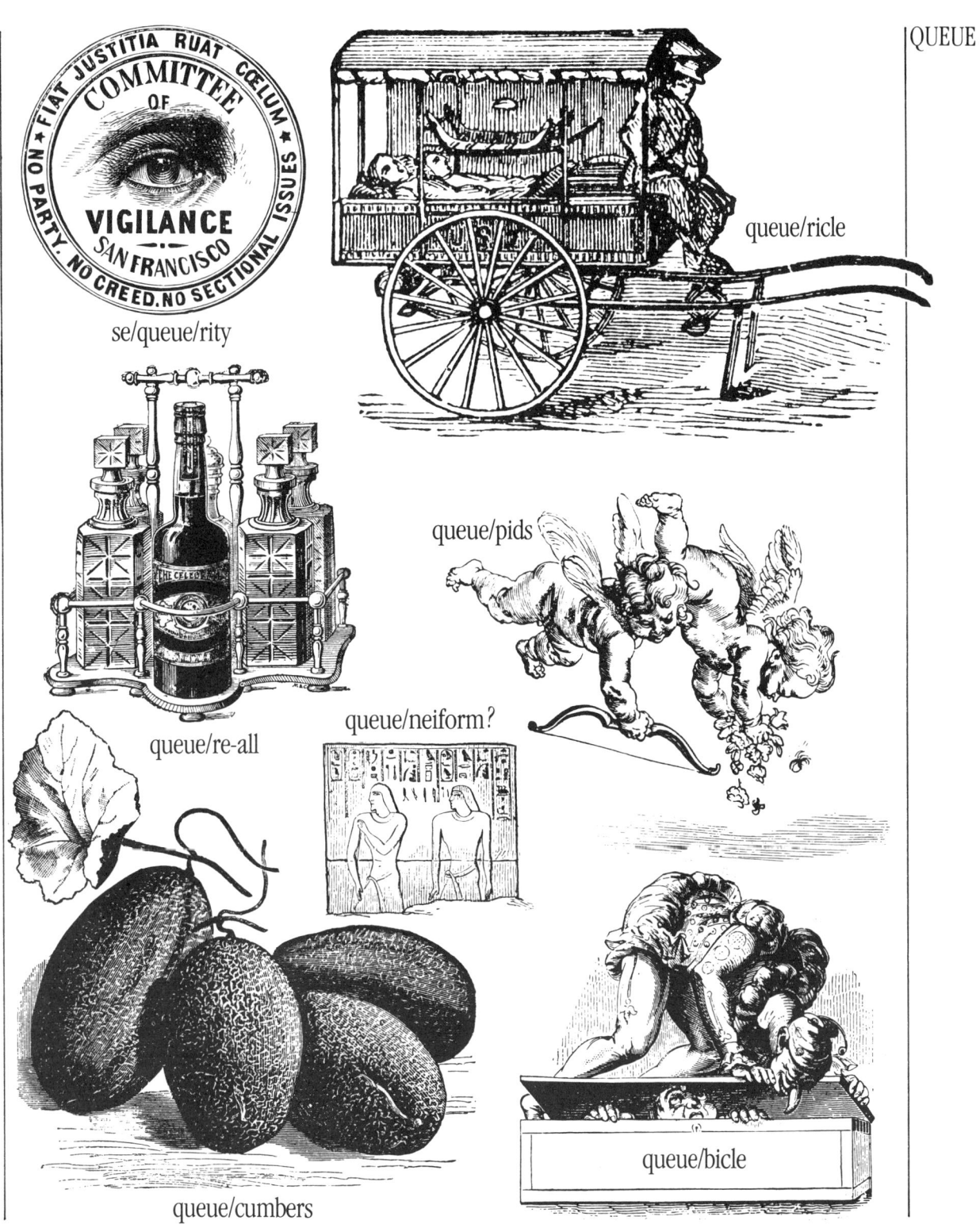

QUEUE

queue/linary

queue/te

Mme.Queue/rie

queue/rator   queue/pola   queue/riosity

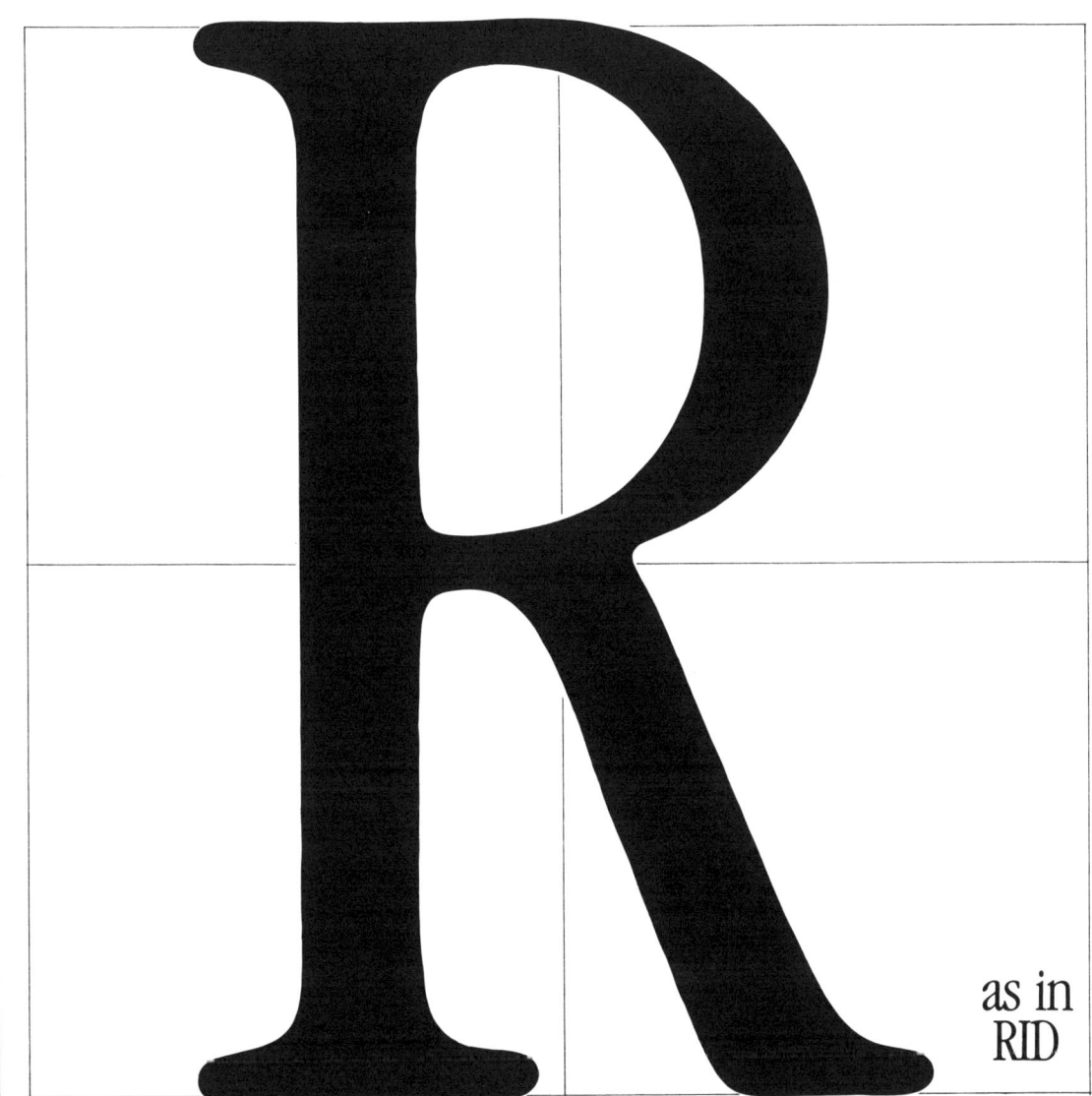

as in
RID

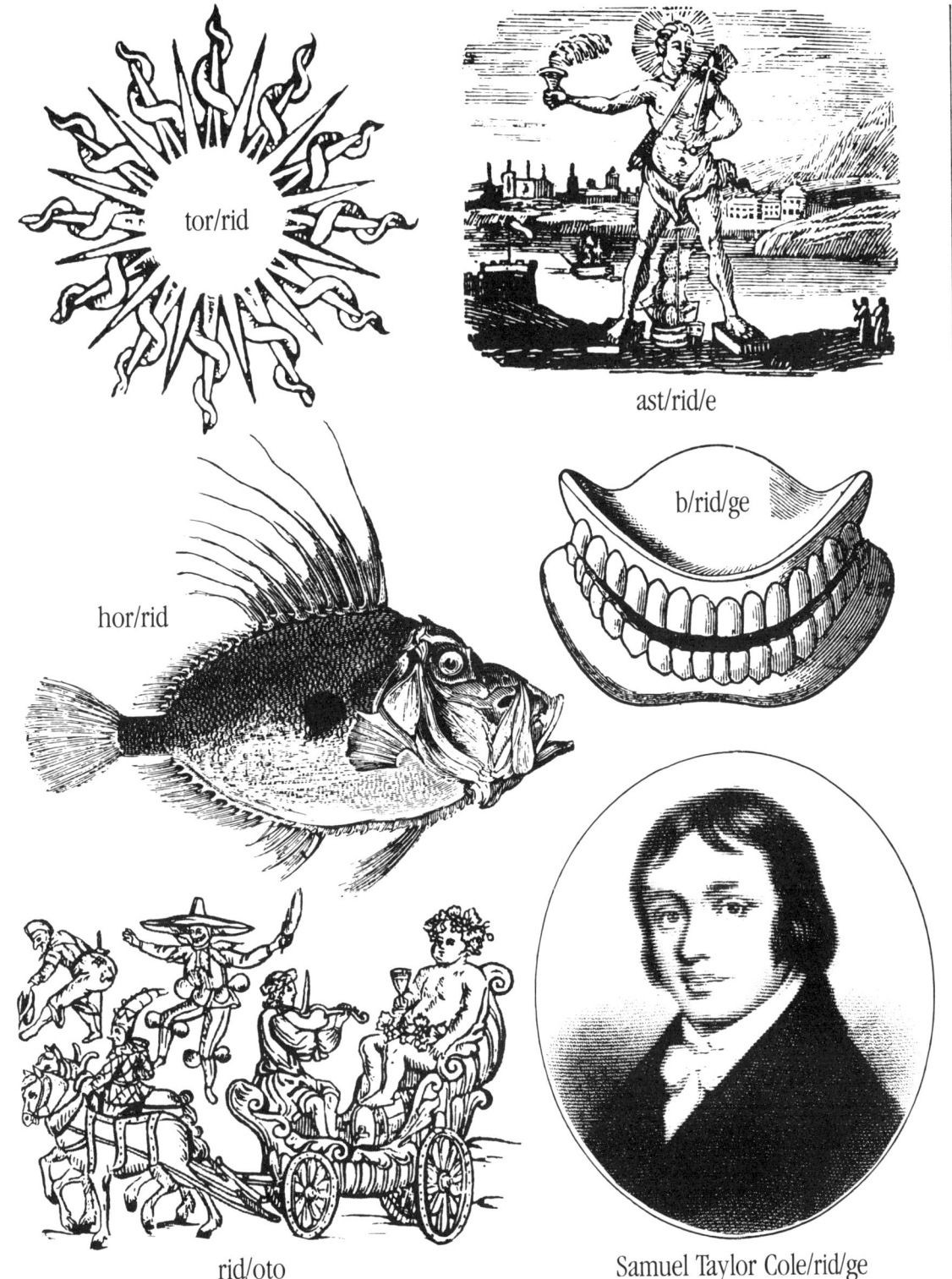

RID

rid/dler

cor/rid/or

de/rid/er

cart/rid/ge

t/rid/ent

b/rid/al chest

as in
SIN

SIN

Sin/bad
sin/ister
sin/ger
kis/sin/g
sin/geing
sin/ker
toc/sin
sin/gle-file

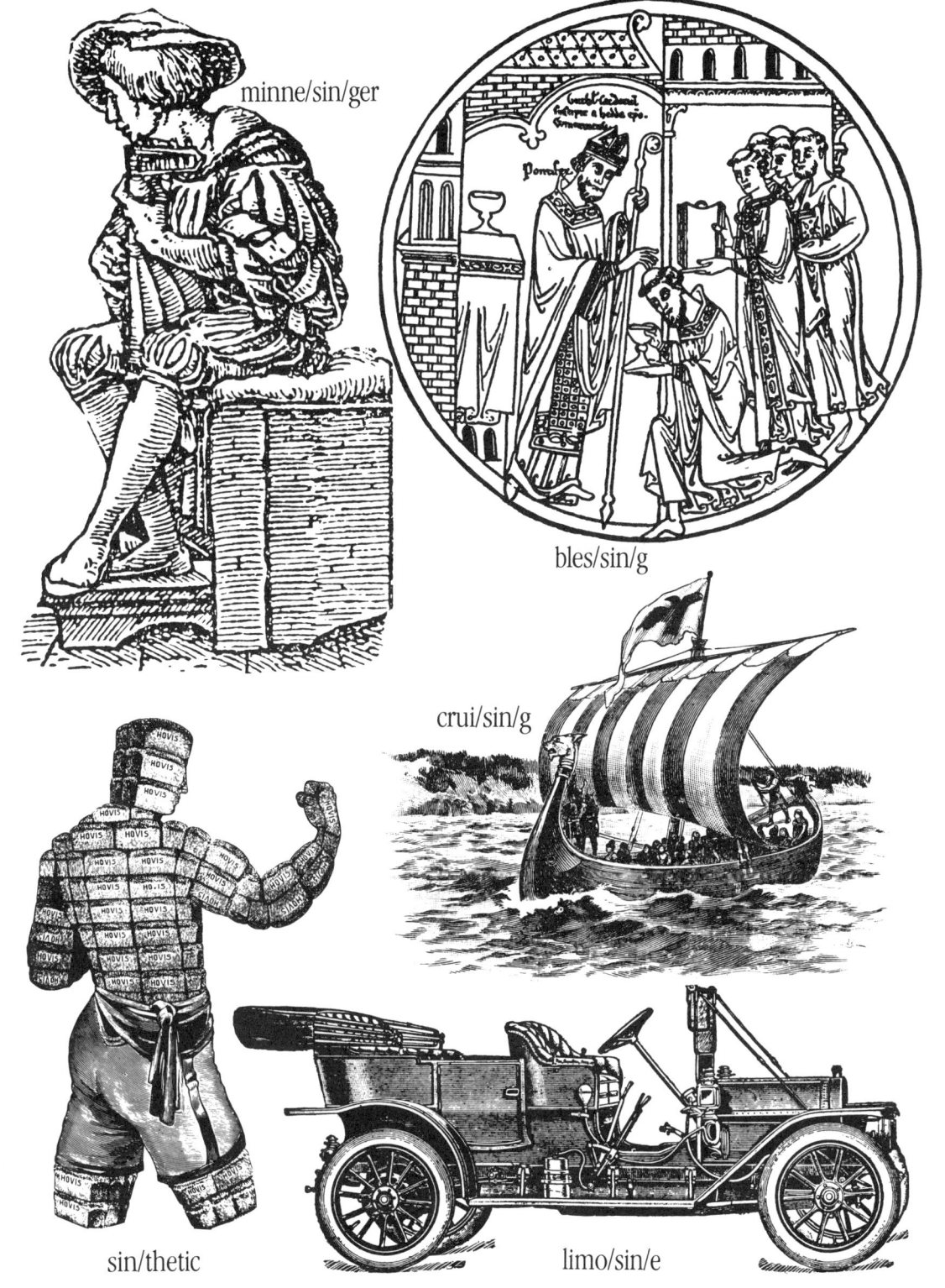

SIN

SIN

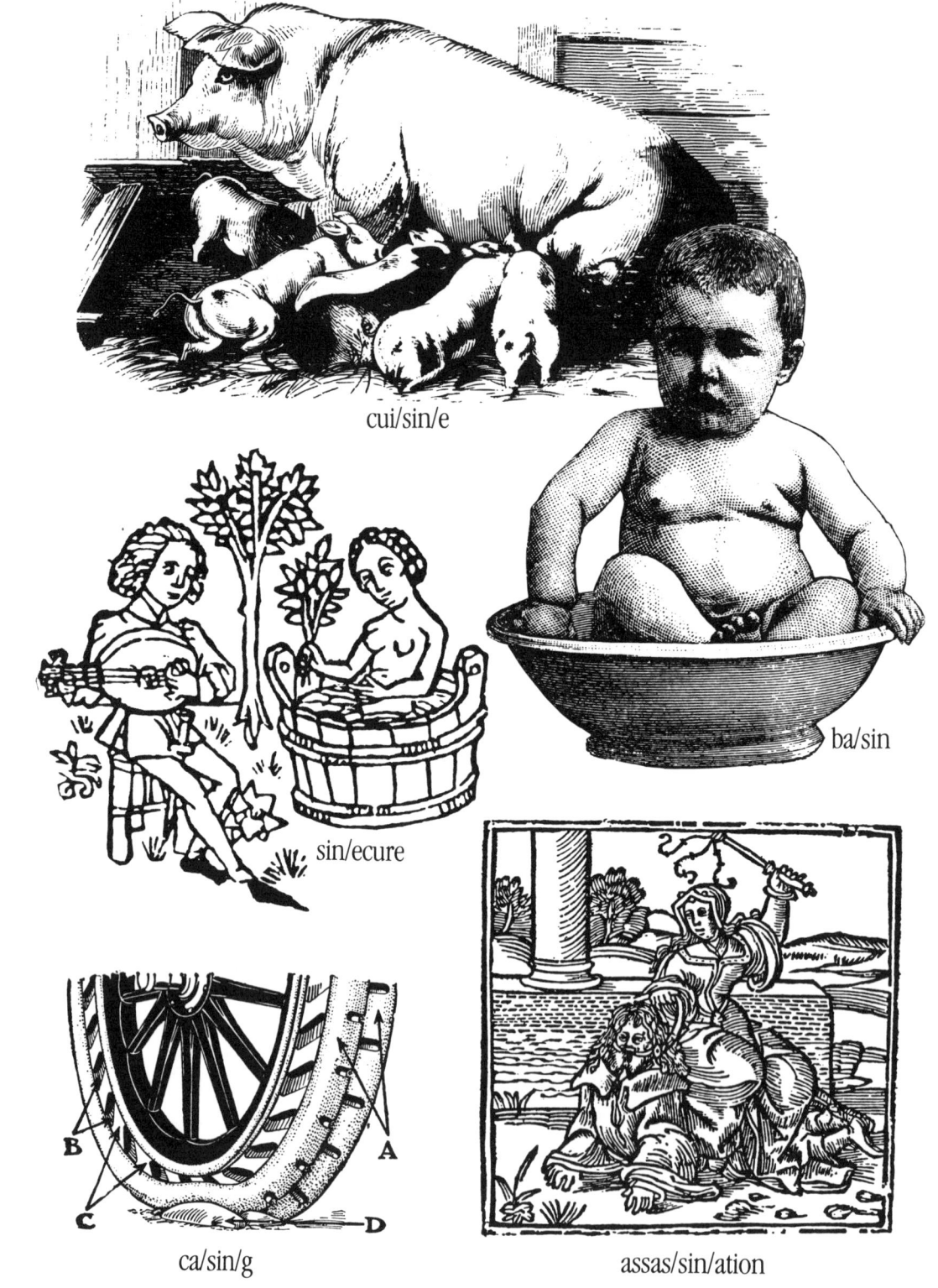

cui/sin/e

ba/sin

sin/ecure

ca/sin/g

assas/sin/ation

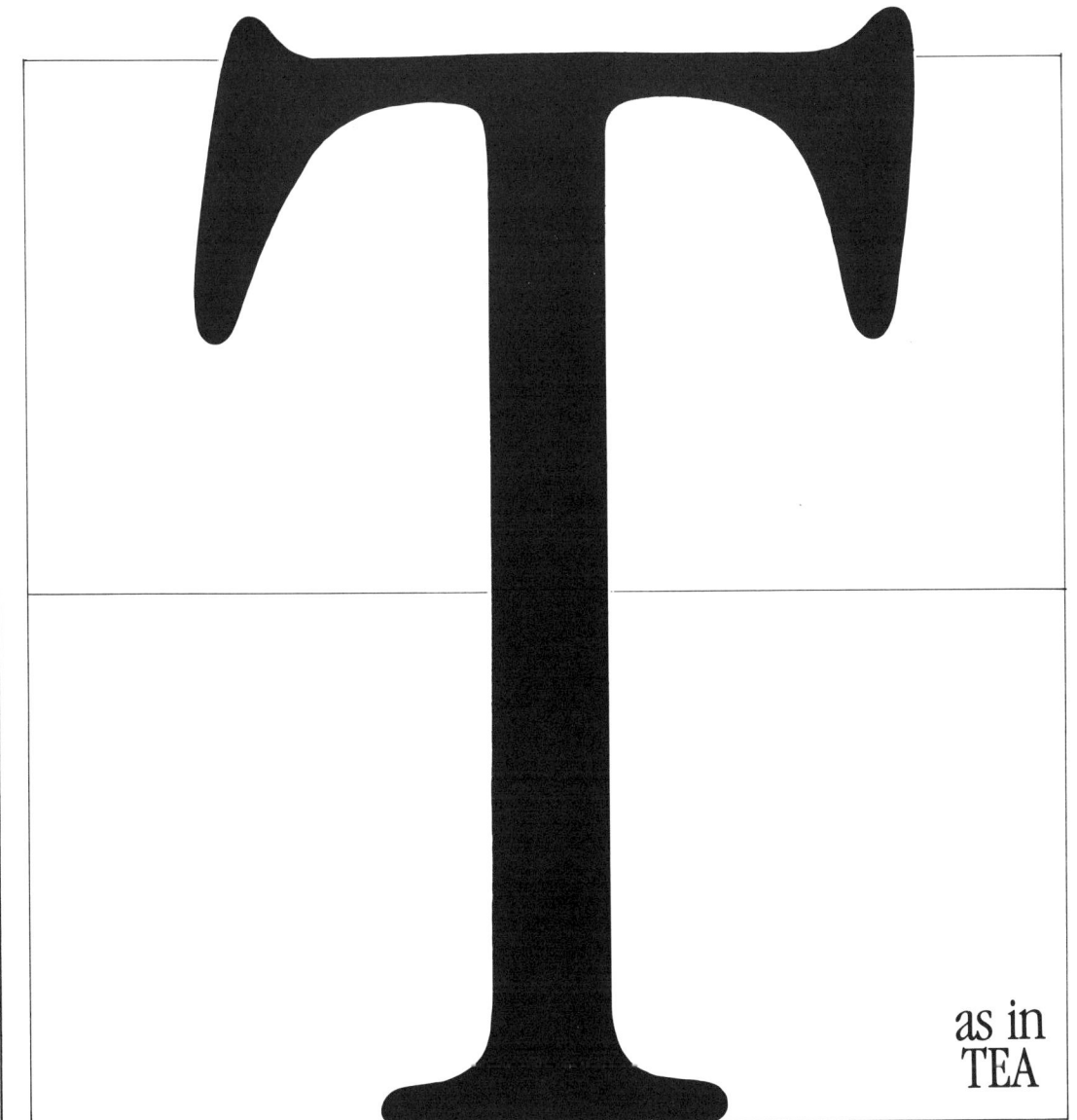

TEA

ba/tea/u
fligh/tea
beau/tea/ful
dir/tea
Tea/Deum
racke/tea/rs

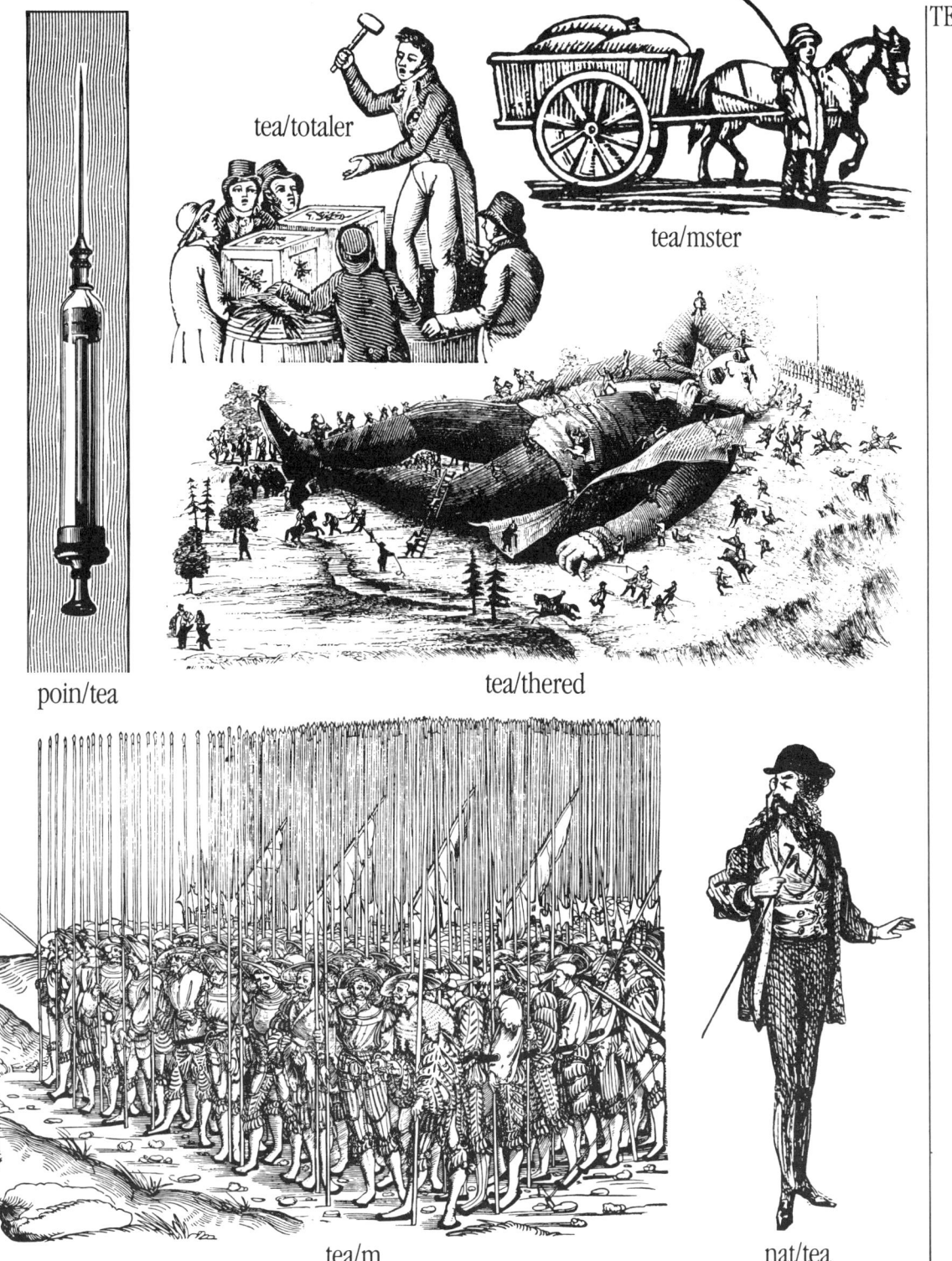

poin/tea

tea/totaler

tea/mster

tea/thered

TEA

tea/m

nat/tea

TEA

weigh/tea

tea/pee

s/tea/ks

goa/tea

gen/tea/l

s/tea/mer

tea/totaller

as in
UP

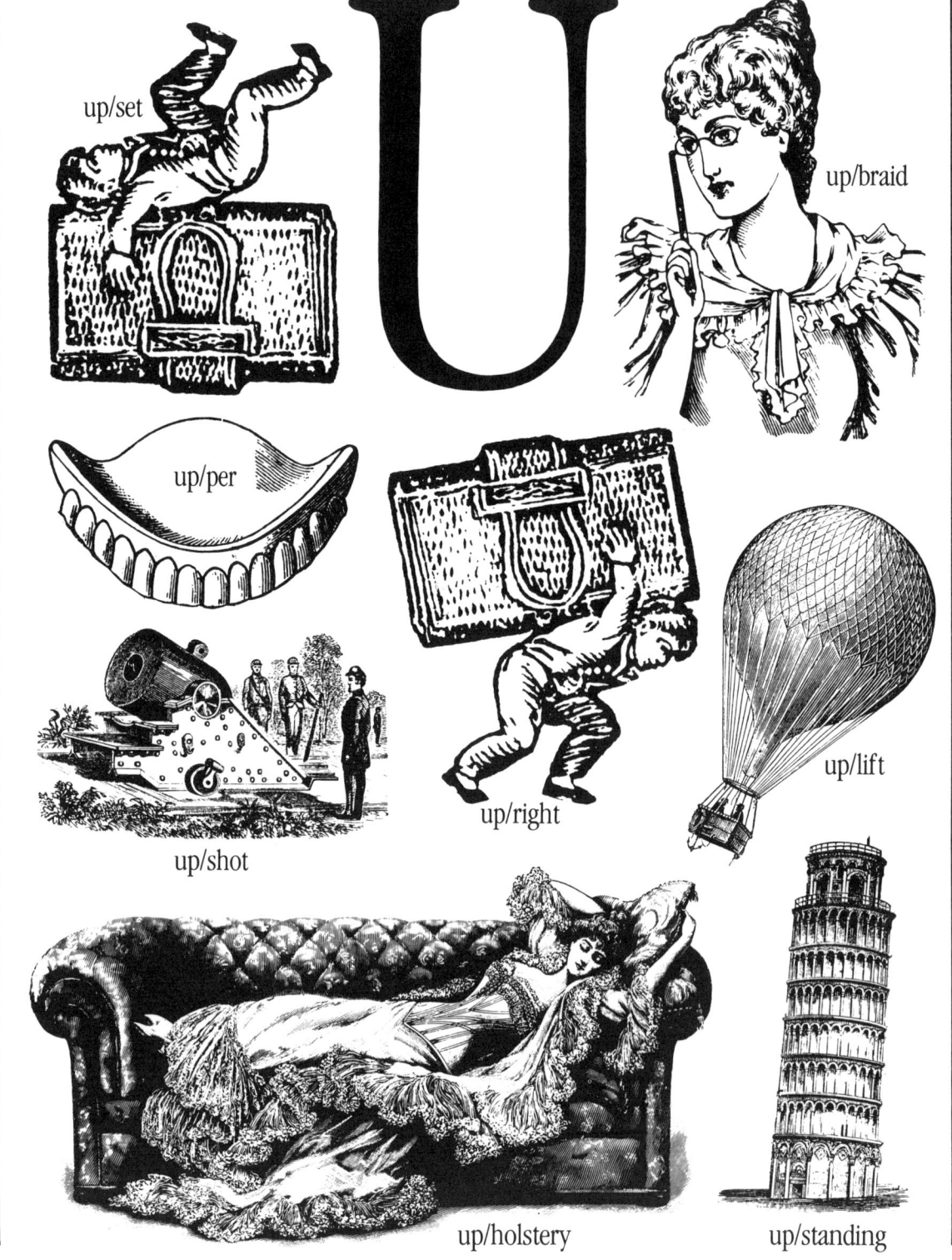

up/roar

up/stroke

up/start

up/heaval

p/up

c/up

leg-/up

UP

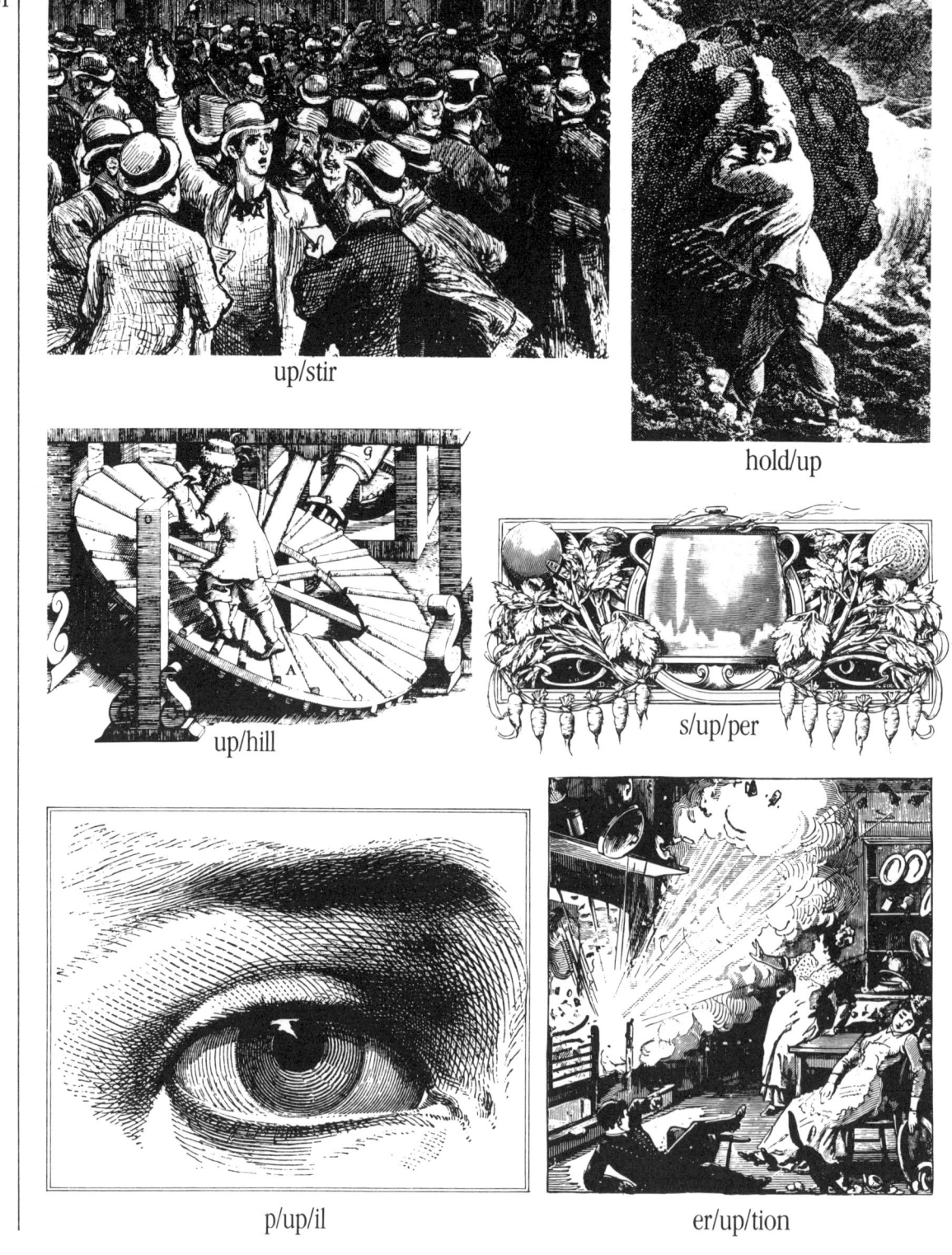

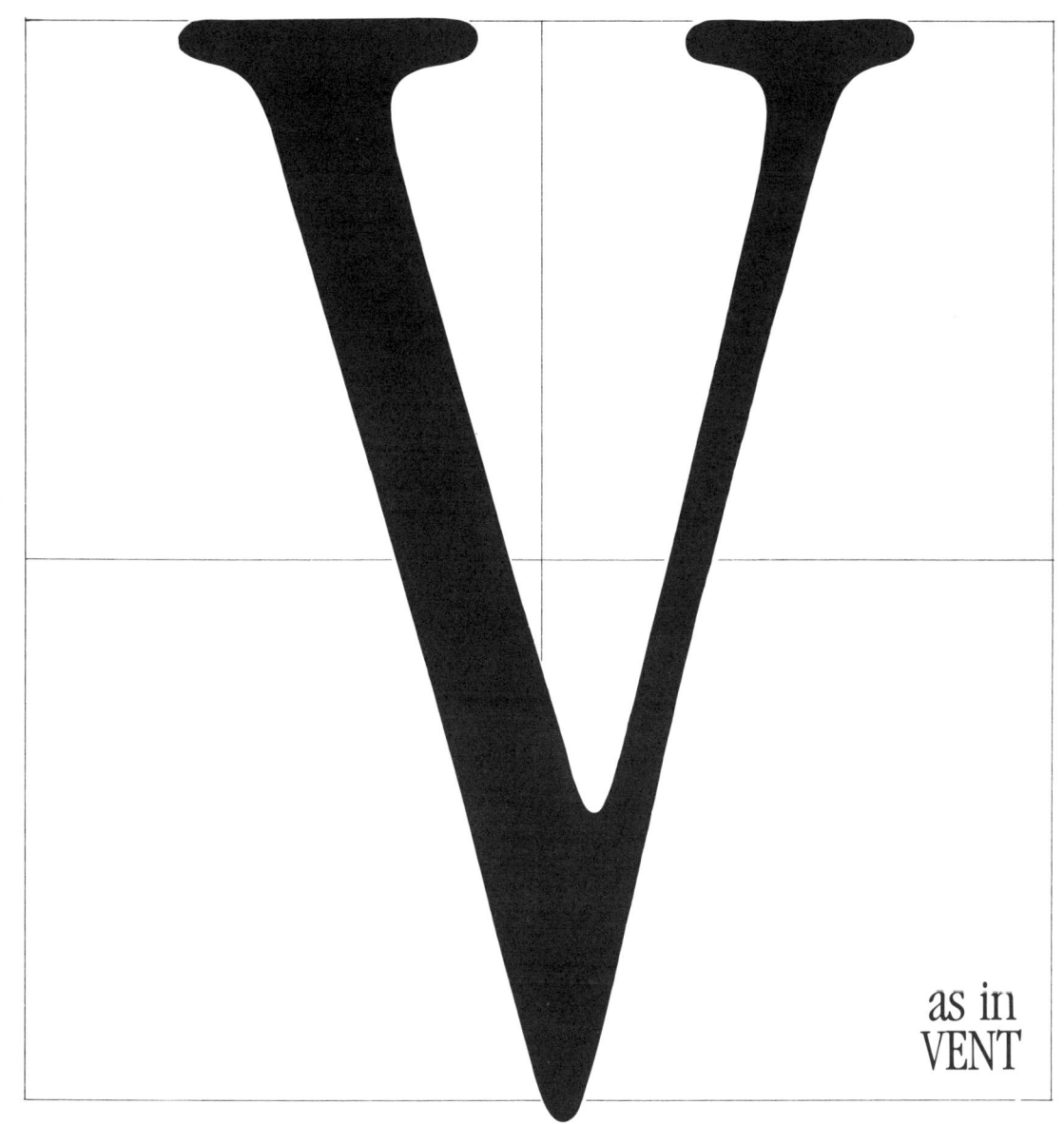

VENT

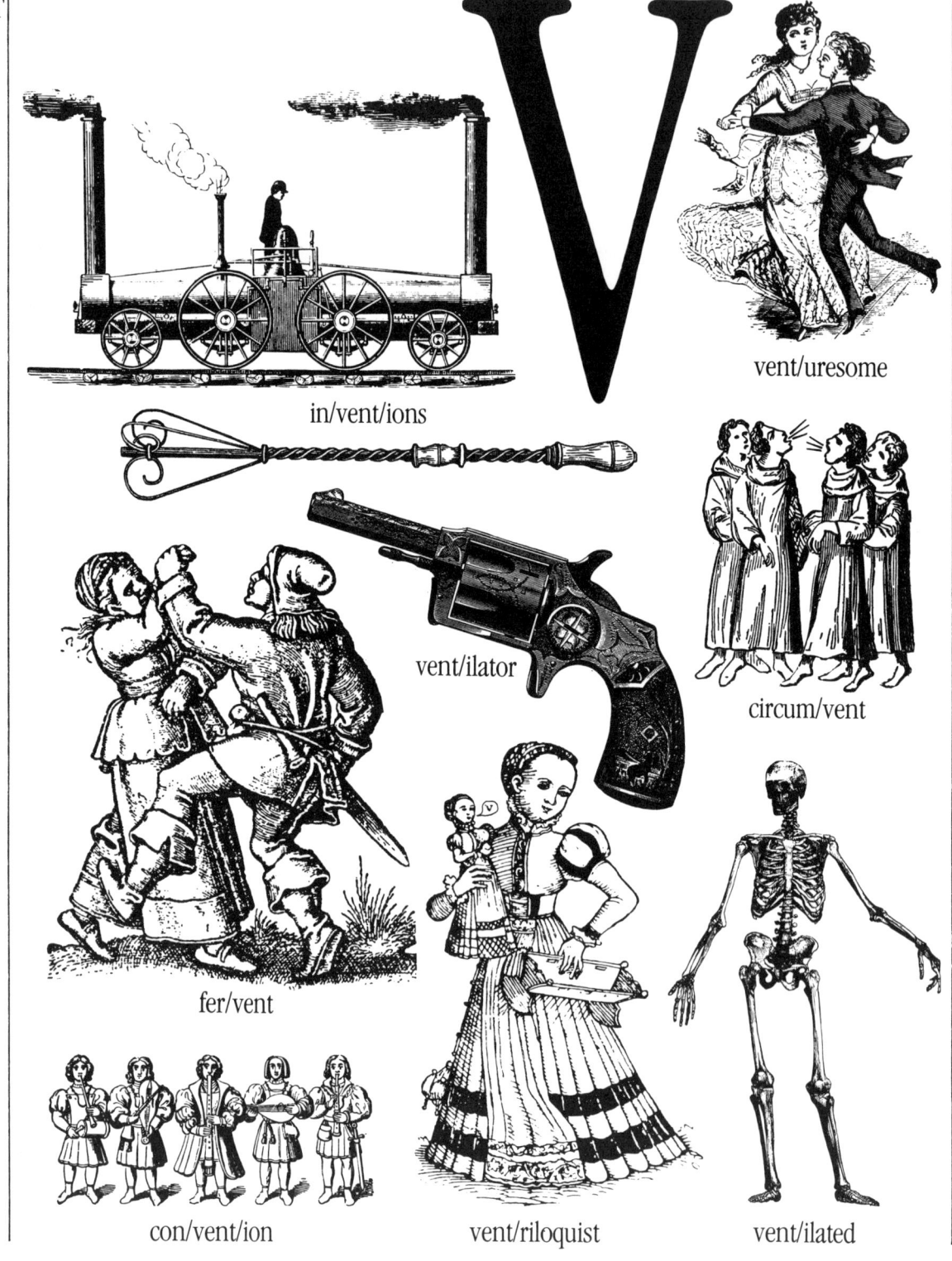

in/vent/ions

vent/uresome

vent/ilator

circum/vent

fer/vent

con/vent/ion

vent/riloquist

vent/ilated

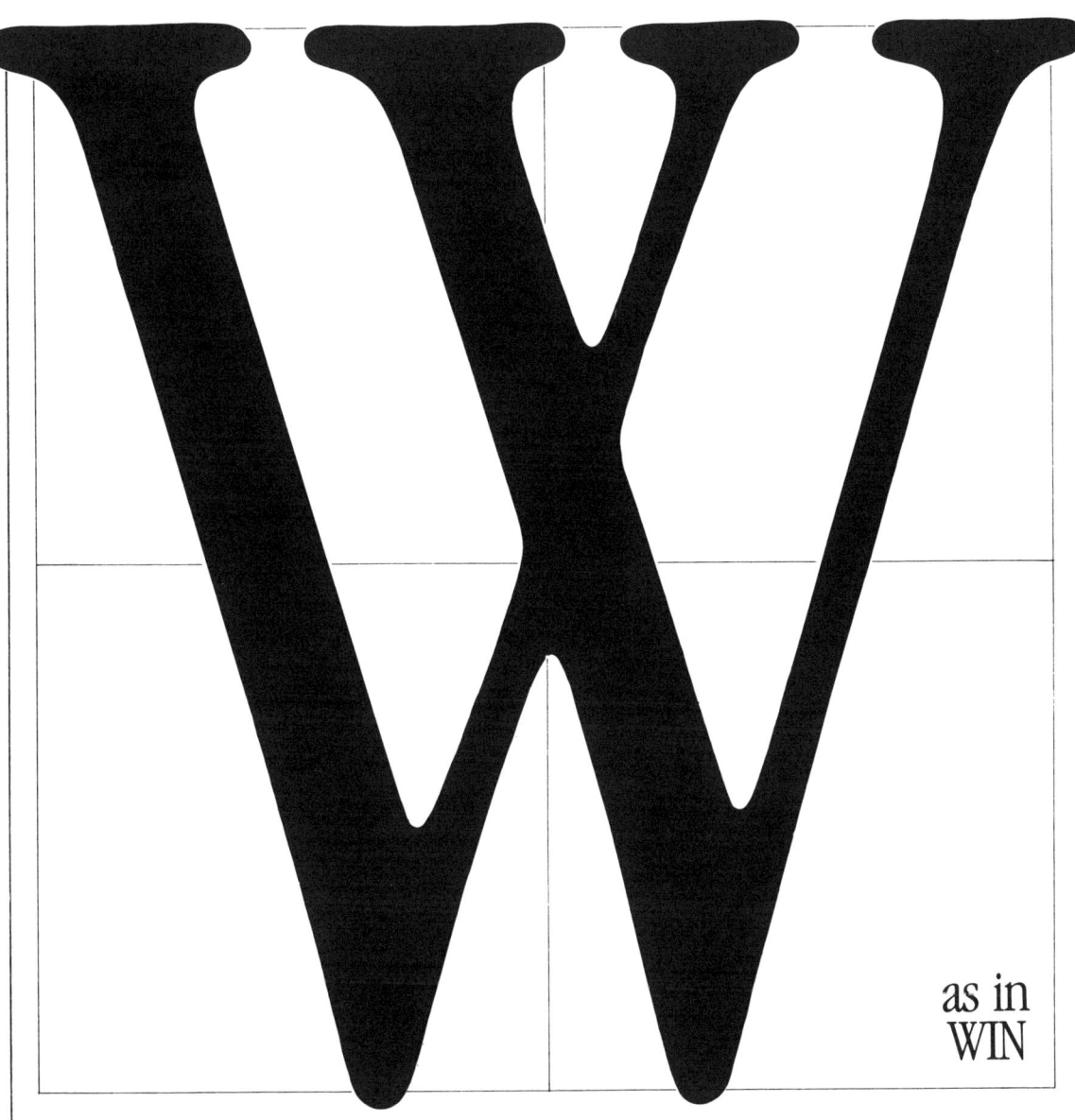

WIN

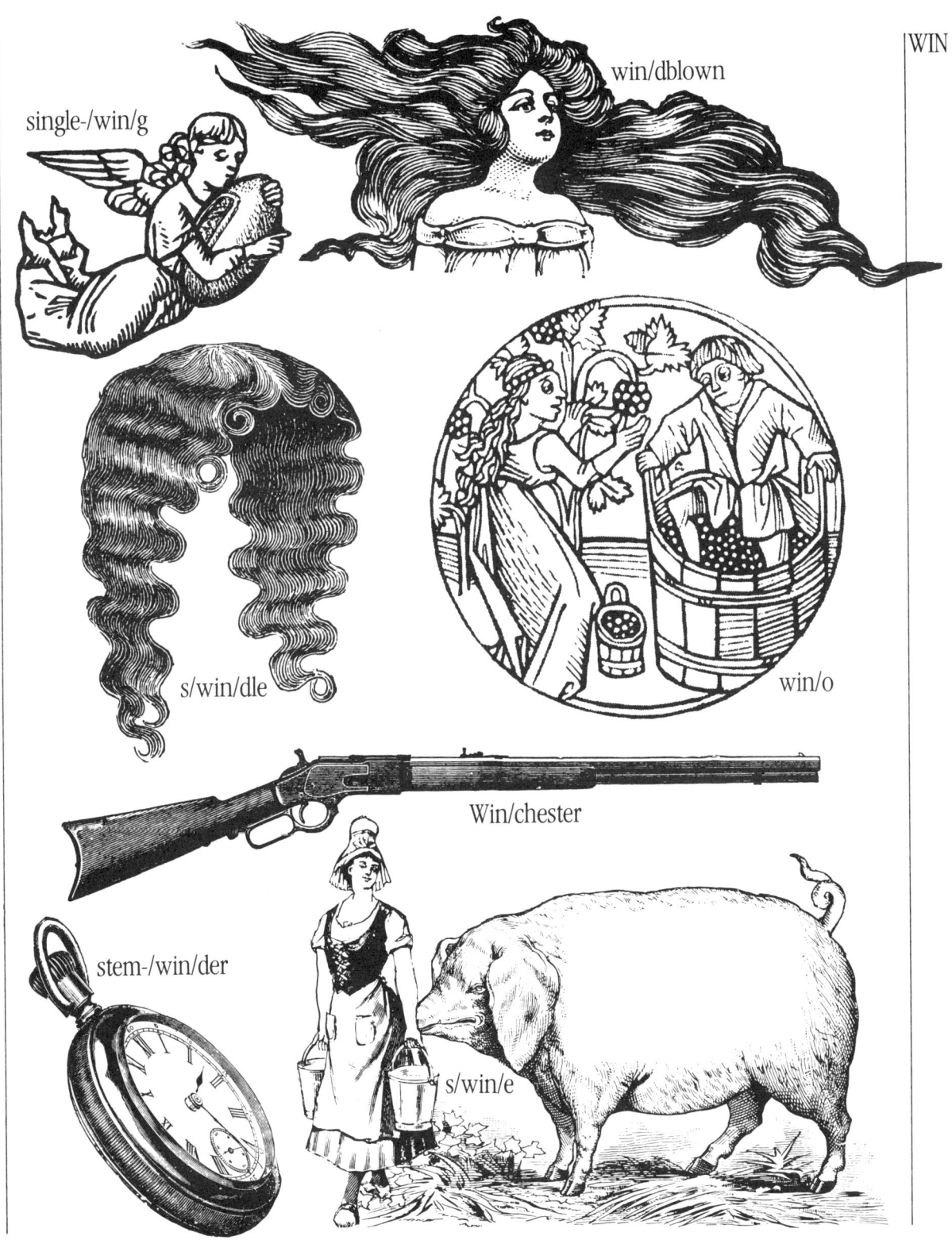

WIN

sto/win/g

Win/ter

down/win/d

win/ch

water-/win/gs

shado/win/g

win/dfall

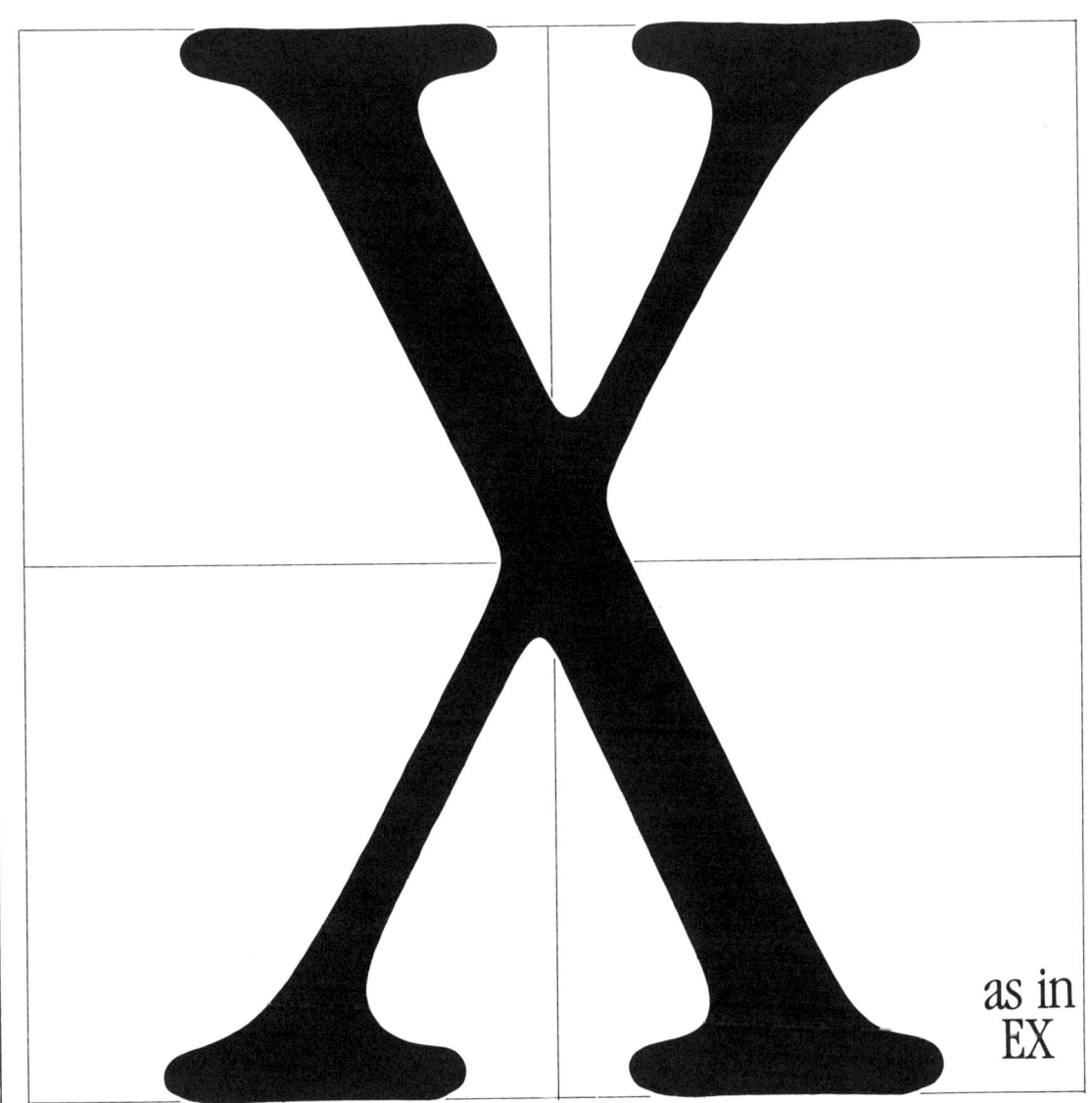

EX

EX

as in
EYE

EYE

Y

h/eye/menoptera

W/eye/f of Bath

h/eye/pertrophy

Duncan Ph/eye/fe

v/eye/al

str/eye/der

h/eye/giene

unappet/eye/zing

modif/eye/r

h/eye/drant

EYE

wr/eye/thy wr/eye/ther

Lord Tenn/eye/son

h/eye/brid

v/eye/ola da gamba

med/eye/cation

Lord B/eye/ron

hippopot/eye/mus

EYE

h/eye/drophobia?

spirit of 'sevent/eye/-six

Pos/eye/don

W/eye/meraner?

t/eye/per

k/eye/te

EYE

P/eye/thagoras

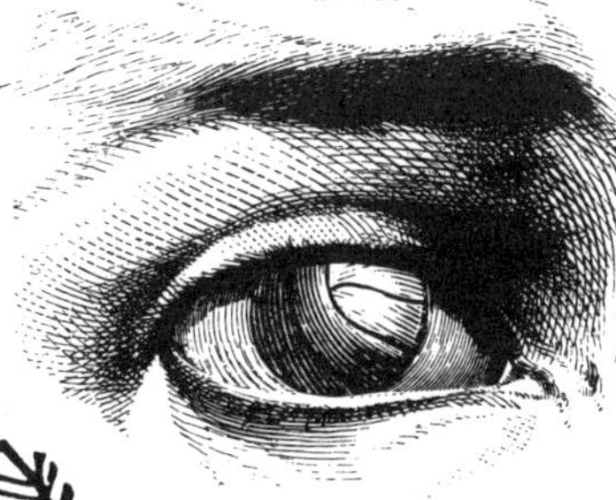

eye/ball

Gustave Eye/ffel

flutterb/eye

fr/eye/ar

tr/eye/ad

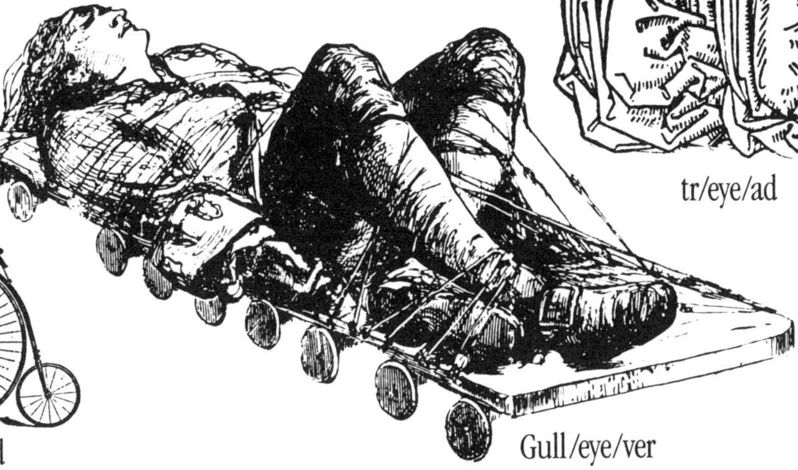

d/eye/ad

Gull/eye/ver

EYE

gel/eye/tin

f/eye/ver

town cr/eye/r

eye/ron man

Franz Joseph H/eye/dn

gr/eye/nder

recl/eye/ner

Bridge of S/eye/s

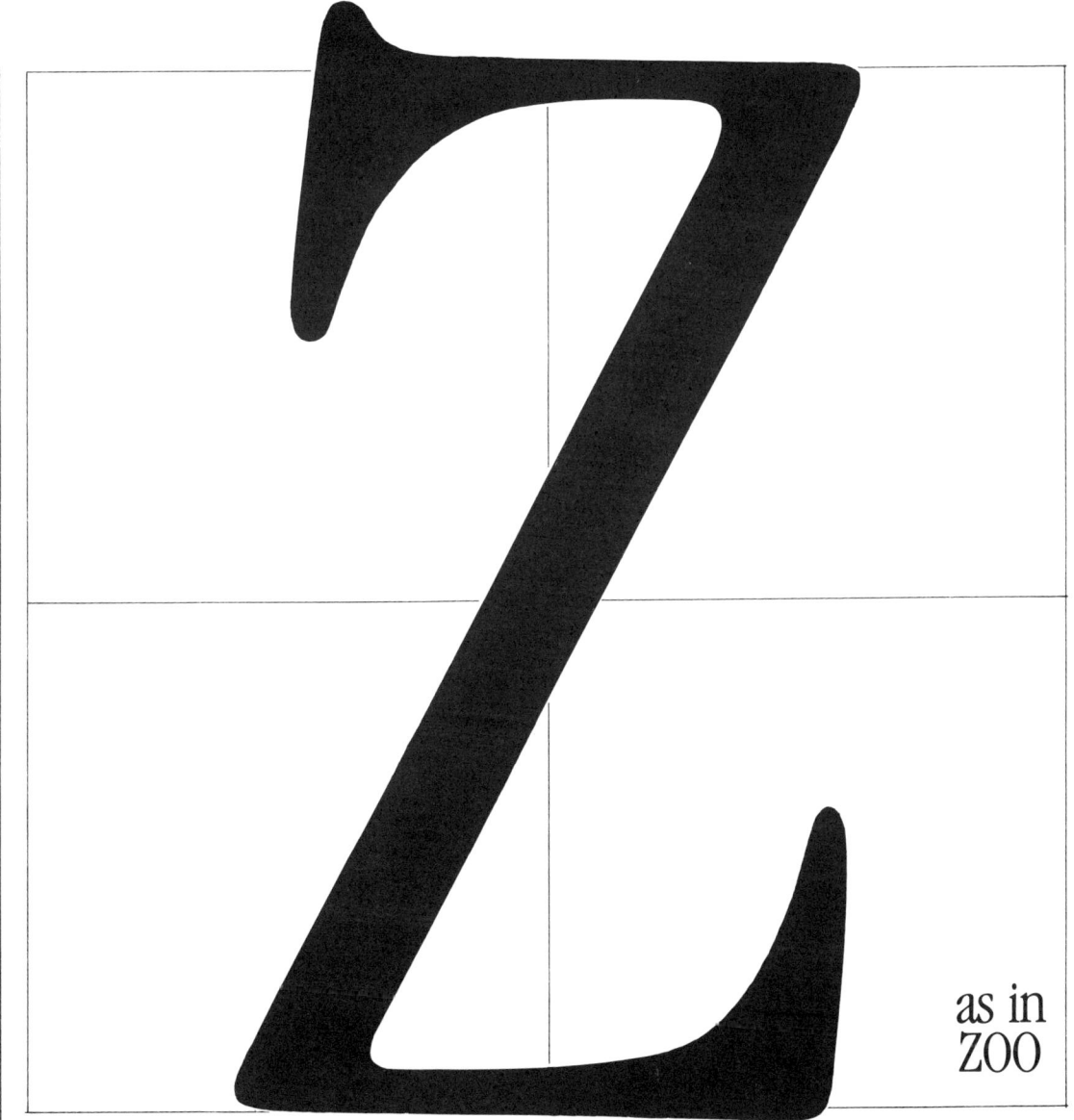

as in
ZOO

ZOO

ZOO

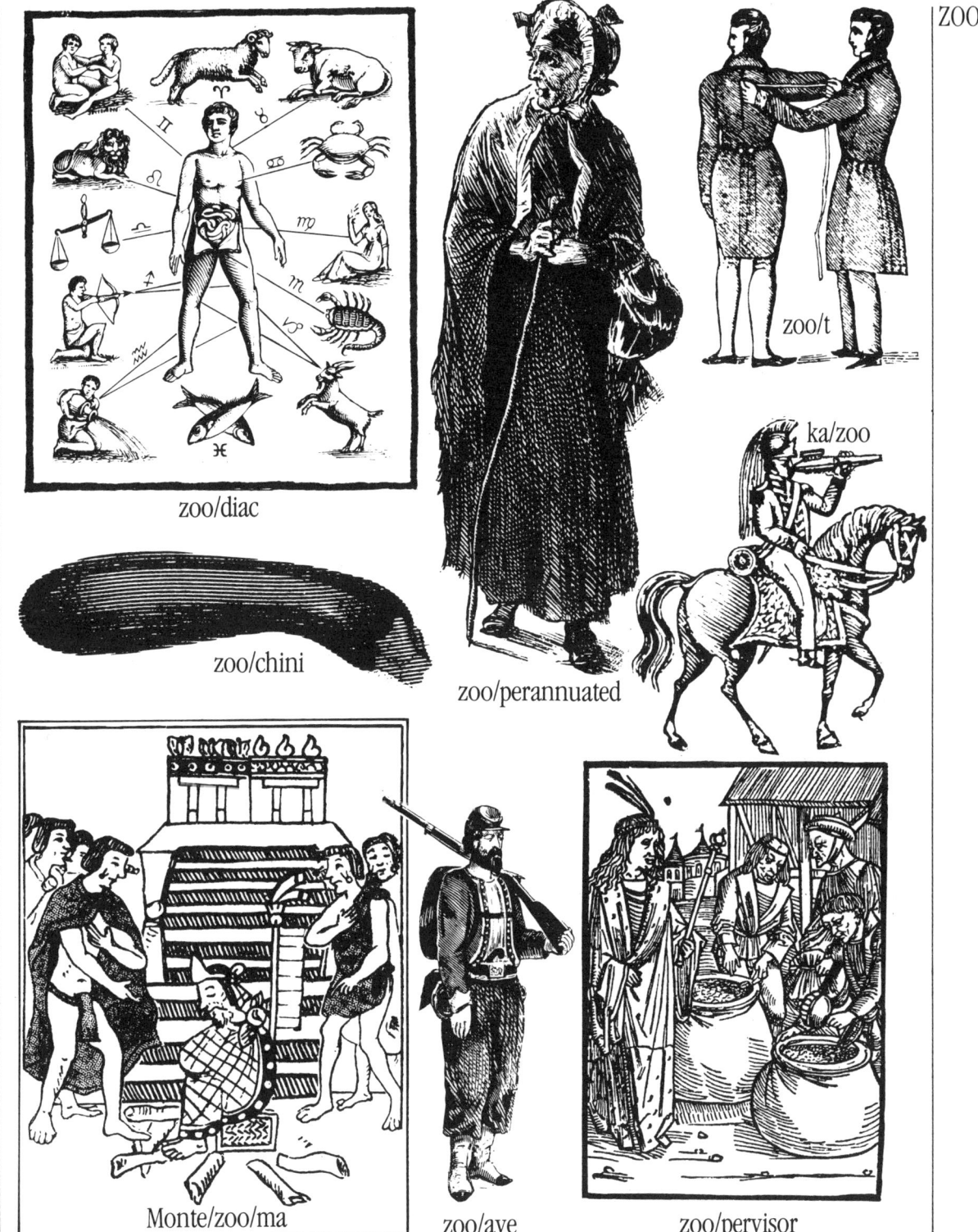

zoo/diac

zoo/t

ka/zoo

zoo/chini

zoo/perannuated

Monte/zoo/ma

zoo/ave

zoo/pervisor

ZOO

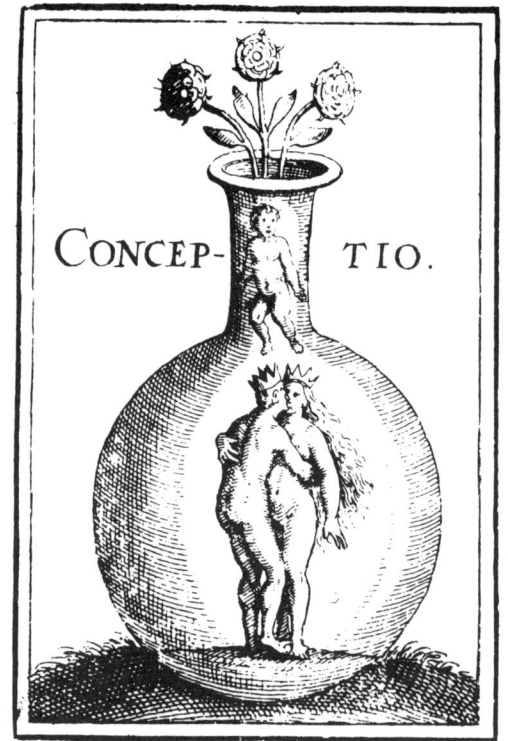
con/zoo/mation

zoo/percilious

zoo/pernatural

Mother Zoo/perior

re/zoo/rection

|ZOO

zoo/perstructure

zoo/perstition

zoo/perimposition

Zoo/preme Court

zoo/prise!

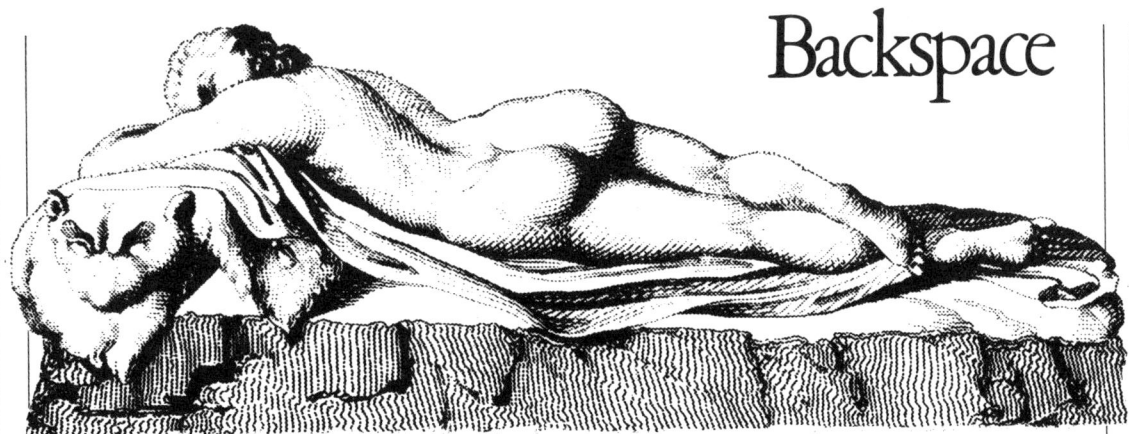

Backspace

Now that the letters have been presented, let us consider how they may be used. Since there are twenty-six of them, if we were to use only one per week, at the end of a year we would have chosen each of them twice; not a stimulating prospect.

However, if we selected them two or three or four at a time (in conjunction with each other), we'd have a different situation; note that when we combine certain letters, strange patterns appear: I and T together form IT… if we preface them with other two-letter combinations, we get SLIT, SPIT, GRIT, CHIT, WHIT and at least one or two more that slip my mind at the moment. Similarly, three-letter assemblages like ART can tag on to other letters to make CART, DART, HART, TART, PART, and so forth.

Thus, whole new possibilities lie before us. Naturally, since there are very few really *new* ideas, there have been some attempts to do something of the sort just described on a commercial basis, notably by a breakfast cereal made up entirely of little O shapes. They, however, have missed the boat. By providing only the letter O, they have limited the possibilities to O, OO, and perhaps even OOO.

If some forward-looking manufacturer is interested, here is a suggestion, provided free of charge, in the interest of the advancement of culture: produce a breakfast cereal in the shapes of *all* twenty-six letters, thereby giving our young people a chance to experiment, for example, with as many four-letter combinations as may occur to them. Perhaps the cereal could be given some catchy alphabetic name (to stimulate sales and thereby letter usage), but that is beyond the purview of this compendium.

Finally, let us remember that the letters have been left to us in trust. If we do not use them, the efforts of all those who have gone before us will have been wasted, and we will become an unlettered people, leaving our heritage to be continued by numbers alone! Imagine a world controlled by the statisticians, bookmakers, actuaries, numbers game runners and certified public accountants. Beware!

Appendix XX

how the letters changed, from Phoenician to Greek to Early Latin

	A	B	CG	D	E	F	H
Phoenician	∀	◁	⌐	◁	⋽		目
Greek	A	ꓐ	>	∇	⋽	ꓞ	H
Early Latin	A	B	⟨	▷	E	F	H

	IJ	K	L	M	N	O	P
Phoenician	Z	⊁	L	W	ᛉ	ʊ	⌐
Greek	⟨	ꓘ	∧	M	N	O	⌐
Early Latin	I	K	L	M	N	O	P

	Q	R	S	T	UVWY	X	Z
Phoenician		ꓞ	W	⊓		王	I
Greek	Φ	P	Ƹ	T	Y	Ξ	Z
Early Latin	Q	R	S	T	V	X	Z

White Clam Sauce

(approximately 4 cups)

1/4 cup olive oil
1 huge garlic clove, minced
2 tbsp. flour
2 cups clam juice
kosher salt and black pepper, to taste
1 tsp. thyme
1/4 cup chopped parsley
2 cups minced clams

Heat the oil in a saucepan, add the garlic and cook over moderate heat. Stir in flour with a whisk, then (still stirring) add the clam juice. Add salt, pepper, thyme and parsley and simmer gently for ten minutes. Add the clams and heat well. Serve over 'al dente' spaghetti, and eat. Please note: chopsticks are required for the proper historical flavor.

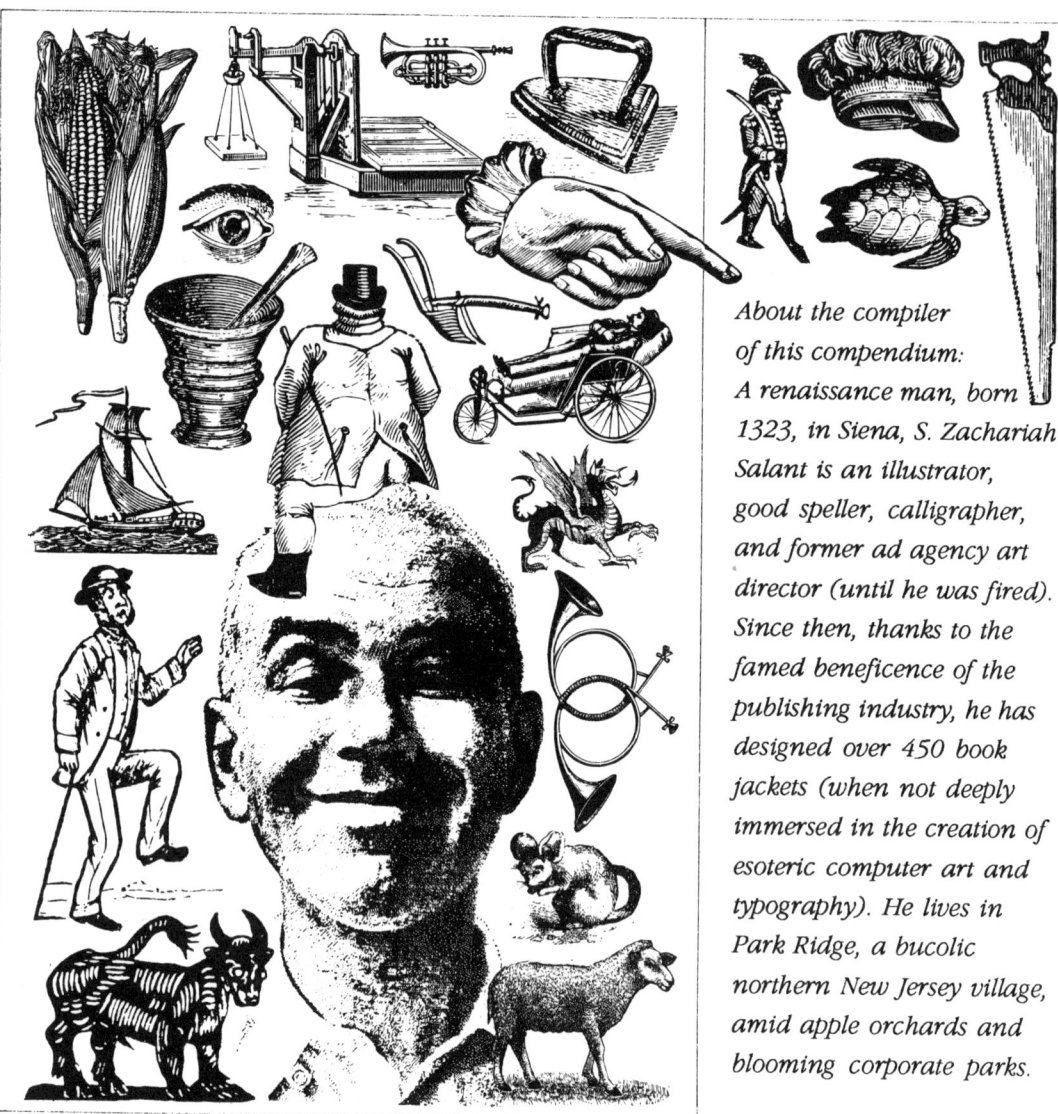

About the compiler of this compendium: A renaissance man, born 1323, in Siena, S. Zachariah Salant is an illustrator, good speller, calligrapher, and former ad agency art director (until he was fired). Since then, thanks to the famed beneficence of the publishing industry, he has designed over 450 book jackets (when not deeply immersed in the creation of esoteric computer art and typography). He lives in Park Ridge, a bucolic northern New Jersey village, amid apple orchards and blooming corporate parks.

Postscripture

This work is written in *Anglish* (after the *Angles,* a Germanic people who conquered the British Isles in the fifth century A.D., and for whom the *English* are misspellingly named). The phototype is *Garamond Old Style* and *Light Condensed,* which are twentieth-century (per)versions of the work of that great sixteenth-century Frenchman of many letters, Claude Garamond.